ABOVE and BEYOND...

JOHN TROYER

Tellwell Talent
www.tellwell.ca

ISBN
978-0-2288-3044-3 (Paperback)
978-0-2288-3045-0 (eBook)

TABLE OF CONTENTS

A B O U T   T H E   C O V E R

The inspiration for "Above and Beyond..." comes from Ephesians 3:20 in the *The Passion Translation.*

> "Never doubt God's mighty power to work in you and accomplish all this. He will achieve infinitely more than your greatest request, your most unbelievable dream, and exceed your wildest imagination! He will outdo them all, for his miraculous power constantly energizes you."

The picture is of EGB when we landed in a hay field near Copper Center, Alaska to visit friends and family.

"A good man leaves an inheritance to his children's children" (Proverbs 13:22). This is the inheritance I leave to my children's children.

ACKNOWLEDGEMENTS

My first thanks goes to my wife, Betsy. She not only stood behind me and encourage me to write this book—she is the one who has always loved me and allowed me to be who I am, but also at times challenged me to stay true to who God made me to be when the pressure was on to conform to another standard. I am grateful!

A special thanks go to our oldest daughter, Faith Gerber, who has loved reading since the time she could open a book. With her love of English—and her patience with me as I misused simple words like "seen" and "saw," "was" and "were"—she has edited and reedited the manuscript every time I changed or added something. Even as she edited, she insisted that I write this manuscript the same way that I talk so that my voice could be heard. Thanks Faith, you are amazing!

Also, a big thanks to Joyce Coy for the first editing of this manuscript, for her patience and carefulness in removing what appeared to be hundreds of my extra commas, as well as the word "so" from the beginning of many of my sentences. The strong encouragement that she gave me was amazing and motivated me to keep it real all the way to the finish.

I am also thankful to the wonderful people that God placed around me. Many aunts and uncles who love the Lord still inspire me; and many close friends have been faithful to God and loved me enough to tell me when I was wrong and at times encouraged me to do right even when it was painful.

CHAPTER 1

Beaver Crossing

1950-1955

T he first home I remember was just outside Beaver
Crossing, Nebraska. It was a two-story house and
I slept in a bedroom upstairs. There were a lot of
boxelder bugs there. They are a nuisance bug that hibernates
in masses during winter in house attics, sheds, and garages,
wherever they can find a hole to enter. They emerge in the
spring to eat the new leaves of boxelder trees. They are black
with red lines on their back and wings. Some people called
them "Democrats." I think most of our family must have been
Republicans. Anyway, my older brother Galen and I used to
catch them. I have heard that mom found some in the toilet,
so she knew we were eating them.

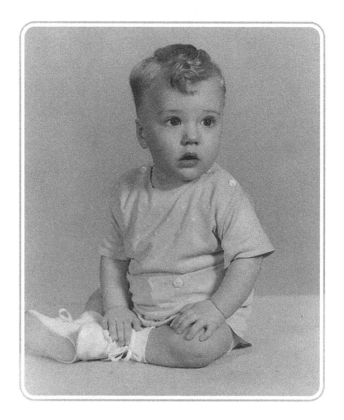

This is me at about a year old.

A few other things stand out to me when I think of living there. One was standing at the top of the stairs crying because I had to go to the bathroom. Mom came and gave me simple instructions, "Come down and go." I don't know why I couldn't figure it out, but maybe it had to do with having a hard time getting "potty trained." I don't remember it, but that is what some aunts and uncles have told me. They also said I fussed and whined a lot, which may have been the case.

During this time, my brother Galen got polio. We visited him in the hospital which had huge, tall, brown doors. I hated going there, but I always wanted to see Galen. It was in this hospital where I heard that eating potato peelings was good for you. Sixty years later I often think of this now when I'm eating baked potatoes! When Galen came home, he had to wear some braces to help him walk, and also one around his chest that held out his arm. I didn't know how he felt about it, but I did not like it when he wore them.

Linda, my sister, also got sick while we lived in this house. After having a very high fever that mom couldn't bring down, she went into convulsions. It left my beautiful little sister with some brain damage that would affect her for the rest of her life. At the time I didn't understand any of what was going on, only that I hated it. Years later I discovered that I was angry at God and the whole world for letting all this happen. Mom must have known how I was feeling because she gave me a book, "Angles Unaware" by Dale Evans Rogers, to read when I was about nine or ten years old. It was the story of her and her husband, Roy Rogers', daughter who had Down's Syndrome. The book made me feel better until Linda would have another seizure; then my anger returned. The seizures were horrible. Mom would be crying and singing while she tried to hold her and keep her from getting hurt. I couldn't understand the "why" of these things. Only recently did we learn that the doctors think she may have had the polio virus in her brain stem. This brought on other "why" questions. There were only three of us children at the time, so why did polio get the oldest and youngest, but skip me?

One other life-changing thing happened while we lived in this house. The atmosphere in our house changed from tense to very peaceful. I was very young, but I remember the feeling. It started when Mom went to a George Brunk revival meeting in Milford, Nebraska, and met Jesus. I can only imagine that the change must have been dramatic, because everything she did was with all her heart. Then several days later Dad went. I've been told that Dad and several men his age only went to "see the girls" and to fulfill their obligation to help usher people into the tent. Knowing Dad's integrity, it's hard to believe this could ever have been possible. They were not allowed to smoke on the grounds, and they complied. That evening Dad met this man named Jesus as well. Later, Dad would say that when he decided to follow Jesus, he knew this was for a lifetime commitment of serving God with all his heart. Knowing Dad like I do, I'm sure he heard the words, "Well done," when he left this world in 2010.

Wedding picture of Dad and Mom, Stan and Darlene

We only lived a few miles from Grandma and Grandpa Troyer, so we went to visit them sometimes. I always looked forward to seeing Grandpa. He had a gold tooth and would show it to us. He would tease us and tell us that whenever we lost a tooth, we could get a gold one, but we would have to hold our tongue over the hole until the tooth came in. I tried, but I couldn't keep my tongue in place very long. In 1955, Grandpa was driving and got hit by a drunk driver. He was killed, and Grandma was very badly hurt.

We would stay in Beaver Crossing with Grandma and Grandpa Oswald sometimes too. Galen and I would play outside in the ditch in front of the house. Whenever I got in trouble with Grandma, she would call me "Johnny Mike." We loved her and didn't try to give her any trouble. She was one of the very few people who I allowed to call me "Johnny."

We had an old-style reel lawn mower that you had to push by hand to make the blade turn. It seemed to fascinate me the way the blade would turn so fast. I don't know what I was doing with it, but somehow I got my right elbow against the blade while I had it turning, and got a big cut. It is a scar that I still carry. My interest, but lack of knowledge, in mechanical things got me in trouble often during my life. Not too many years later, when I was around ten years old, I would take the head off the Briggs and Stratton engine on our power mower every time I used it, just to clean off a bit of carbon. Dad would find out and tell me not to do that because it didn't need to be cleaned, and I was going to ruin the head gasket by taking it apart so many times.

CHAPTER 2

Cairo

1956-1964

We moved to Cairo when I was in the first grade. Dad was working for my uncle Lester driving truck. Then Dad got into farming, rented a farm a few miles west of town, and began farming. It was in the Sand Hills, so the soil was very sandy and dry. We milked cows and had sheep, chickens, and pigs. It seemed there was always something to do as we grew up. We had to gather the eggs from the chicken house. I hated this job because it seemed like the eggs were always really dirty. A few of the chickens would always cackle and make lots of noise when we were in the chicken house. It seemed to me like they were bragging.

One day one of them came out of the chicken house, cackling, and wouldn't shut up. I picked up the closest thing to me which was a bone from a round steak. It was the perfect shape, like a flat stone. I threw it at the chicken for all I was worth. I hit it in the neck and it just flopped over kicking and flapping like its head was cut off. I ran over to it and tried to make it stand up, but its head just flopped to the side. Afraid that Mom or Galen had seen me, I grabbed it and ran to the outhouse and stuffed it down the hole. No one ever said anything about it, so I didn't either.

I remember the challenge of getting the milk pail high enough to pour it into the strainer on the milk can. Later we poured it into the cream separator. The cream got sold and the skimmed milk got fed to the pigs. Often before the cows were all milked, Dad would suggest we make ice cream. We did this often, so Galen or I would stop with the chores and go make ice cream. Since we had lots of cream and eggs, Dad and Mom made very good ice cream. It is a known fact that Dad loved ice cream, and we learned from him that ice cream is always delicious.

We had a lot of skunks at this place. Galen and I would chase them, but we always stopped in time when they turned around to face us. We knew they couldn't spray us while running away. It was when they stopped to face us that we would be in trouble. One winter we had a skunk in the calf pen in the barn. We had to go in there and give the calves milk; of course, we were very nervous the whole time! After a few days it left, and things returned back to normal.

Dad was farming some hay fields around the area, so we had to drive the tractors on the road. This was a lot of fun and a good excuse to drive "wide open" as we called it. We learned that we could hook our toes under the governor lever of the John Deere model B and pull it back. The tractor would really rev up and go. It's a wonder we didn't blow up an engine. Dad bought our first new car while we lived here. It was a VW bus with a 4 cylinder, very underpowered engine. My cousins, Ron and Don, made fun of it and said it couldn't even get up to 60 miles per hour. I couldn't believe it was that bad, so I waited for my chance to try it.

I was probably in the sixth or seventh grade when my chance came. I had driven the tractor to the field and Dad followed later with the VW. He wanted to open the field and start mowing; so he had me drive the car a couple miles back to the house. Our lane was at the bottom of a fairly long hill and I thought this would be the perfect time to try and "hit 60." Away I went. At the top of the hill I floored the gas pedal and glued my eye on the speedometer. Up it climbed, slow and steady, and when it finally hit 60, I looked up to discover that I was very close to our lane. I didn't know much about driving so I put in the clutch and pushed on the brakes. It was as hard to slow down as it was to speed up. For some reason, going past the driveway wasn't an option in my thinking at that time, so in I turned. The driveway was at a bit of an angle, so I made the turn without hitting the ditch and then went flying down the lane.

Mom was just coming out of the house and her hands went up to her ears as she watched me. I sped past the house, yard light, garage, barn, corn shed, and out into the field of corn before I got stopped and turned around. Slowly, I drove back to the house and parked feeling very satisfied that I had proven my cousins wrong. I knew it could "hit 60." I remember getting a serious talking-to, but I think Mom talked even more seriously to Dad because I don't ever remember getting to drive the VW again.

While we lived at this house, God began to influence me in ways that I didn't understand. It wouldn't be until years later that I would understand what God was beginning to shape in me. I was about eight or nine years old during this time and would have a recurring dream. It was always the same. In the dream our whole family would be in bed sleeping. I would hear a knock on the door, but nobody would get up to answer it. So I would get out of bed, noticing the clock showed just after midnight, and go to the door. Standing at the door were four men that I recognized as prophets and apostles from Bible times. They would come into the house and talk while I sat and listened. I never spoke. They would get up and leave at sunrise and I returned to bed. When I would wake up after having this dream, I felt so alive and connected to something bigger than life.

But while God was working to shape me in His way, there were other things working to take me away from God. One of them was a very bad temper. I began to resist authority at school and fight with others who I felt were taking advantage of me. I was often in trouble. School was easy so I didn't have to work hard to get good grades.

While we lived here, Dad was chosen to be the pastor of the Mennonite church we attended. I didn't like this, but I don't remember why. The man that Dad was renting the farm from didn't like it either, so he told Dad that we would have to move. He was not going to have a preacher living on his farm. Dad never told us this until years later.

Our next move was to Dannebrog, a very small Nebraska community north of Cairo. The small school was only a couple miles from our house. I was in the seventh grade. The time in school did not go well. I got hit a lot by the teacher for laughing when I wasn't supposed to and telling jokes that were just a bit off colored.

The best part of living there was that Uncle Gary and Aunt Lela often came to visit. He taught me how to shoot a shotgun and hunt pheasants. Gary gave me one of his guns, a 12-guage single-shot. But things didn't go well for Dad that year as there was no rain. So the crops failed and there was no money to pay back the Farm Credit Loan that he had taken out in the spring for seed and fertilizer.

I remember when three men from the Farm Credit came to visit and wanted Dad to sell some cows to pay off the loan. Dad didn't want to because we needed to sell the milk to buy food. They talked for a long time and when it was over, Dad decided to sell out and move back to Cairo. He had found a place that was irrigated so he could farm and not have drought kill the crops. Dad sold everything except a few cows. When we moved to the farm a few miles East of Cairo, Dad went to work at the sale barn for the winter. This was an auction barn where farmers brought animals to be sold. I started attending a country school that fall. It was only a mile or two from the house, so we road our bikes most of the time. While it was a different school, different students and teacher, my behavior was the same as before.

CHAPTER 3

Back to Cairo

1964-1967

The move to Cairo was complete and school started that fall. I was in the 8th grade which was the highest grade in that country school. There were only two classrooms; in my room there were grades five through eight. We had one teacher for all these grades with about 20 students. I didn't like the teacher right away, and it was obvious she didn't like me. I quickly made friends with another troublemaker named Jimmy.

One day the teacher warned all the other students to avoid doing anything with me because I would only get them in trouble. I was surprised she would say that, but I remember thinking that this was a challenge to take on and give her something to talk about. Resentment against authority grew a lot that year as she and I worked to get the best of each other. One day she planned a square dance for a Friday activity. I was determined to not even try and do it. At that time, I was not going to be holding hands with a girl or putting my arms around one. This did change later in life, but at the time it was only repulsive. After many threats, the final ultimatum was that I would either dance or not get to participate in the softball game the next Friday. Angrily, I went through the motions.

Another time she told us to make up a story about anything we liked. We were to write it down and hand it in the next day. Since I had always liked to watch airplanes fly over us, I decided to make up a story about flying. It was about two young men in a small airplane. They had trouble with the engine while they were flying and couldn't get it restarted. I wrote about them leaning out the windows and trying to adjust things on the engine while they were flying. (Now that I'm a pilot, I can see that most of it would have been impossible to actually do.) I added all kinds of other details that would have been absolutely impossible in real life, but it made an exciting story with lots of drama. To finish the story, I had them landing cross ways in a corn field and walking away like it was all normal. I handed it in, satisfied that I'd written a good story.

The teacher thought otherwise. The next day when she handed the papers back, she stopped at my desk and said, "This is the worst thing I've ever read. Where did you ever read something like this?" She had drawn a big red line across it. After showing it to me, she crumpled it up and threw it away. I was hurt, angry and disappointed. Years later as I tried to start writing this book, I would read what I wrote and hit the delete button because I was sure it was no good. Thankfully, I have friends that talked me through this block and encouraged me to write and not judge it as no good.

As the year ended, the teacher was getting everyone ready for the exams that we had to take before entering high school. We needed to go to Grand Island for the day of exams. The teacher was telling us that she expected certain ones to do really good because she had taught them for the last several years. They were her favorite students as well. When the exams were finally taken and scores in, she was not happy. I had gotten the highest score in the class. She never said any more about her special students. My grade eight ended with the same hostility that it started with, and I was glad it was over.

High school was pretty much a repeat of the last couple years of grade school. I didn't have to study to get decent grades, so most of my time was spent goofing off. Math was my favorite subject; the others subjects like English and History seemed to be filled with a lot of useless information. One year the guidance counselor suggested I should take Chemistry because the year before Galen, my older brother, had gotten some sort of award. I could not convince him that Chemistry was not for me. It took about a month or two before they realized that the teacher was wasting his time and mine. They finally let me out of the class when my grade average was about 4 or 5% out of 100%. That was the year they started a class called, "Social Problems." All of us in the class thought it was a very interesting name for a class until we looked around at who all was in the class. It finally dawned on us that we were the "Social Problems." Our teacher didn't seem to be very stable, in our view anyway. She would frequently burst into tears and leave the classroom. Sometimes she would send us to the principal's office with a note. We would usually open it and read it before leaving the classroom. The notes were usually the same, something like, "I'm sending (fill in the blank) to you because his behavior is deplorable." Thankfully for us, the teachers were not allowed to hit us anymore. I don't think they knew what to do.

In August 1965 just before starting back to school, Galen and I were in a car accident. A car hit us broadside and we all ended up in the hospital. My pelvic bone was cracked in several places. We spent about a week in the hospital. It was no fun, and the memory of waking up with the car on its side bothered me for a long time. I thought I was dying because there was blood coming out of my mouth and I couldn't breathe. The radio was blaring the song, "Going back to Houston." I finally started breathing, but Galen and the others were still out cold, so I crawled out over top of them. They all started waking up shortly after I got out. For the next few months, I had some serious thoughts about life and even tried to change. Somehow, I always got back into the same anger and hatred.

I enjoyed fixing things, so when I was fifteen I bought a 1955 Ford. The automatic transmission was worn out, so I took it out and replaced it with a standard. That meant putting in a clutch petal, all the linkage along with the clutch, transmission, and a different drive shaft. Thankfully, there was a junk yard only a few miles from home, so Dad and I often went there to get parts. The car was ready to go when I reached 16 years old and got my driver's license. I put some nice big tires on the back, and it looked pretty nice, even though they were implement tires, rated at forty miles per hour maximum. They actually held together at 100 mph and squealed really easy when I spun them on the pavement. All the work done to this car really messed up the speedometer, so I played ignorance while talking my way out of a speeding ticket shortly after I got my license.

I split the exhaust, so it had "duals." We used a straight through bullet-shaped glass pack muffler that sounded pretty nice. We learned to amplify the sound and percussion by running a garden hose up the exhaust pipe when the muffler was hot. The cold water would shatter the fiberglass mat in the muffler so it would blow out. It sounded loud and powerful. I loved to show off when I would leave for work at the butcher shop during school hours while all my friends were still in the last study hall. As I would leave the school parking lot and drive onto the gravel street, I would "floor it" as we said then, and gravel flew all over the place. The sound echoed all around the school area. It was all so fun until one day just before leaving the study hall, the coach, who we all feared, walked over to me and said, "If you spin any more gravel on the street when you leave here, I will make you pick up every piece by hand and put it back in place." I started leaving a lot quieter and didn't spin any gravel after that.

With the freedom that goes with having a car, the opportunities for getting into trouble really increased. I started going to some pretty wild parties and making very bad choices. I never had an accident, but by looking at the car tracks the next day, we knew that we narrowly avoided disaster. My friends and I would vow to be more careful, but we never were.

Home was still stable and secure. We still milked cows and farmed. I wanted to quit school and often complained that I'd rather work than be in school. Mom and Dad would never give in to me. They told me later that they did finally reach a point where they decided that if I complained one more time, they were going to agree with me. Thankfully, the Lord stopped my complaining, so I never quit. In spite of my secure home, my temper usually dictated what I did. More than once I really wanted to hurt Galen, but he would outrun me. I can never remember what the issues were.

Once when Mom was doing laundry, my wallet got left in my jean pocket. My driver license got destroyed. When she discovered it, she told me right away and said she was so sorry, she didn't know how it happened. I got so angry and said some terrible things to her. She just stood there and cried, but I couldn't stop shouting. This memory has caused me more pain than all the other things I ever did wrong. It was over 30 years later that I finally started to find some healing. It was after a long talk with Dad when I told him about this and how much it still hurt when I'd think about it. He told me that he knew what I was talking about because he had some of the same kind of painful things to deal with. His main comment was, "I know that God could keep us from doing things that would cause us so much pain, but He doesn't. He just brings His Grace alongside us, and it changes our character."

We moved off the farm while I was in the 11th grade. Dad bought a shop in town and started doing mechanic work. I loved being in the shop with Dad and often went there after school. During the summer before grade twelve, I started working at the grocery store's butcher shop. On Saturdays I would butcher whatever animals came in; sometimes it would be a cow or two, sometimes a pig. Once someone brought in a sheep. I knew where to shoot cows and pigs with the 22-caliber rifle, but I didn't know where to shoot the sheep. The manager of the meat department told me the best way to do it was to just stand over it, lift its head, and slit its throat. Since I considered myself fairly tough, I knew I could do it. Little did I know that God was starting to reel in the net for my soul. I stood over the sheep, lifted its head, and pulled the knife around its throat. The blood flowed across my hand, but the sheep didn't even flinch. I heard the words, "Like a lamb that is led to the slaughter, and like a sheep before his shearers is dumb, so He opened not his mouth" (Isaiah 53:7). My knees went weak, as a picture of what Jesus did for me was visible there in the slaughterhouse. I had heard Dad preach about what Jesus had done for us, but it never made any sense, until seeing this sheep bleed and die in silence.

The late nights out partying with friends continued, and I kept looking for ways to come back in the house at night without making any noise. Often it was 1 or 2 a.m. and I didn't want anyone to see me or hear me. I would turn off the car's engine a block or so before home and coast in, usually very satisfied that I didn't make any noise. But I'd be surprised from time to time when Mom would say something like, "You must be tired today after getting in so late last night." Then one day I overheard a conversation between Mom and my aunt Jeanine. Mom was telling her, "I know John can't figure out how I know when he comes in because he is so quiet. But I refuse to get into bed until he is home, so I stay on my knees praying for him until I hear he is in." God was reeling in the net, and the nights out sinning with my friends began to lose their thrill after that, because I knew Mom was on her knees beside the bed praying and waiting.

CHAPTER 4

I Meet the Lord

1967

The evening started out like many other evenings in our small town. We had just finished up the school drama production, "Arsenic and Old Lace." I was one of the actors and all of us were happy that we were finally finished with it, even though it had been a lot of fun. Now we celebrated by driving up and down main street in our little town, honking and waving at each other, smoking openly but keeping the beer hidden in the trunk. We would get it out later.

Somehow during our driving around, I ran a stop sign. The town cop just happened to see me, so he pulled me over. My anger came to the surface very quickly as he wrote out the ticket. He just stood quietly by as I told him what I thought of the stop sign; then I continued on letting him know what I thought about him, his mother and all his family. As I started to get more agitated, he informed me that he was arresting me and taking me to jail for the night. We would face the judge the next day. I told the girl that was with me to take the car and go home. I got in the police vehicle and was told that since I was not yet 18 years old, we would be going to talk to my dad first so he would know what had happened.

It was about 11:30 PM as we pulled up to the house. The family was just getting home from the revival meetings at church. The evangelist, Melvin Paulus, was staying at our house so he was with them. The whole scene made me angrier. I went into the house to get Dad to come out to talk. I was instructed to tell Dad the whole story, which I did, giving all the ugly details. Dad had always been very understanding and helpful when there were problems, so I thought he might offer some solution to my situation. But he turned to the officer and said, "Well, I have done all I can for John, now you take him and see what you can do with him." I felt like Dad had totally let go of me and I was on my own. As brave and angry as I was, I started to get afraid of myself. My anger was totally out of control and I was afraid. Something must have shown because the officer told me that if I could apologize for all I had done, he would let everything go except the stop sign violation. I apologized with no feeling. Later, he took me to get my car. I drove directly home and went to bed.

As I woke up the next morning, it was with resolve to do better. I would go to church and look good, but I determined not to go forward and give in when the invitation was given for those who wanted to get things right with God. I was sure that bringing God into the picture wouldn't work for me; it never had before. Our church was small with an aisle only down the center. The benches went all the way to the outside walls. Since I was afraid of what I might do when the invitation was given at the end of the meeting, I sat in the back row all the way against the outside wall. That way it would be difficult to get out. I tried not to listen as Melvin Paulus preached. He preached Jesus and all He had done for me. It seemed like it was only for me that Jesus came. If that was true, then He could change me. I got up banging and bumping every knee that was in the way as I worked my way to the aisle and down to the front. I was miserable, broken, sad, and tired; not sure if even this would work. Melvin and I talked for a long time that evening as I reached out in faith towards God. I went to bed that night wondering if this would actually work.

The house was quiet the next morning when I woke up. I just laid there for a minute wondering what was happening. I couldn't understand the peace in my heart, no anger, and no feelings of revenge. Was this the presence of God in my room? It was a peace and rest I had never known. Excitedly, I became aware that this WAS His presence in my room. This moment in my life became an anchoring time in the years ahead when times were difficult. If God could do it once, He could do it again. And He did!

My graduation picture, spring of 1968

Change came slowly. Often I went back to the old way of living in spite of the Grace given to me. Always I returned and found forgiveness. It troubled me that I would so easily choose wrong, but it amazed me that God would keep bringing me back. I worked hard to stay right with the Lord. My biggest disappointment came one Saturday evening when Dad and I were working in the shop. Dad had finished rebuilding an engine in a truck. It was cold outside, so the door was only open when he ran the engine to make adjustments to it. Then it was shut again. I was changing a starter on another vehicle. Neither of us realized that the shop was filling with carbon monoxide. Dad started acting very strangely and when I playfully pushed him sideways, he fell over and started talking weirdly, in a high voice. I drug him outside and the man who owned the truck followed us. Running back inside, I called the doctor and told him what was happening. Back outside the truck owner was acting the same way dad was, so I ran back inside to call his wife to come and get him. That was the last I remembered, but his wife said I called and in a very high voice tried to tell her what was going on. When I woke up, there was an oxygen mask on my face. Dad and a fireman were bending over me calling my name. The next hour or so was very difficult, and I learned the painful details later. Finally, everyone left so Dad and I went home. We determined not to tell Mom because we didn't want her to worry about us. When we walked in the house she looked at us and asked, "What happened to you?" Dad played down the whole thing as no big deal. I went off to bed. The next week our local newspaper, "The Cairo Record," ran a front-page story of the event in our shop. After Mom read it, she had another conversation with Dad. Poor Dad! We knew she loved us all.

The next week I learned of my behavior during the short hours after the firemen left the shop. I was not functioning well due to the effect of carbon monoxide. Some of my friends who were there laughed and said that I was babbling a lot and about every other word was a swear word. I felt horrible when I heard them talk. How could this happen after I gave my heart to the Lord? It took a few years for me to learn that change in our character comes slowly, but with God it WILL happen.

I Remember
(Written in 2011)

It was 1968 and life was dark. The shadows in my eyes made everything appear darker than it was. Life was a cruel joke to be laughed at, mocked, and challenged. If there was a God, He appeared at times to be indifferent. At other times it looked like He entertained himself by watching his creation struggle to survive the unjust life He forced us into. I remember the confusion and anger and rebelled against everything because I saw no light. The destroyer was doing his job and I lived in hell.

I remember the adrenalin rush of doing risky things; it was like a pill that dulled the pain of hell. But hell always returned. No hope, no life, no love, and no God.

Then Jesus came! I remember the night He came and changed it all. He took the shadows from my eyes and I saw for the first time. There was a God: He cared! When I saw the sacrifice, I knew I was loved. It wasn't for the world; it was for me He died. I met Jesus. Late that night as I went to bed, I fell asleep at peace, no longer in hell. Next morning I awoke and remembered Him. Life was new and I could see light.

Memories remained and often would almost send me back to the destroyer, but I would remember Jesus, and stayed in His light. At church we'd sing, "Precious Memories," but I couldn't sing it. Most of my memories weren't "precious." But then I'd remember Jesus and hell retreated again.

Now the hell of the past is only a distant memory. God never took it all away. He left just enough so when choices were made, there was an understanding of what turning back would bring. Now I live with Him and choose to stay.

The memory of that first meeting in 1968 is still fresh; it never faded. His love is still overwhelming. His life still keeps the destroyer away. Now I choose to know Him in the power of His resurrection, because I remember.

CHAPTER 5

Big Changes

1967-1971

High School graduation marked the end of many things for me and I was ready. I was still trying to live as a Christian and having lots of difficulty finding freedom from who I had been and the influence of my old friends. The Vietnam War was in progress and the draft was still in effect. In July 1968 I turned 18 so I had to register for the draft. There was a problem. After spending the last four years resisting all authority, fighting, and partying, it would be hard to prove that I was a conscientious objector.

When I went to Grand Island to register, I carefully and respectfully filled out all the appropriate forms and left. Within a few days, dad told me that he had heard that Northern Light Gospel Mission in Red Lake, Ontario, was looking for someone who could help with mechanical repairs. I liked the idea right away. It would get me out of Nebraska and put me in a context where I could grow in my relationship with the Lord. It was a volunteer position and only paid $20 per month; but food and housing were provided. (I learned later that Dad and Mom paid my support the whole time I was there.) It would also satisfy the Draft Board as a place where I could fulfill my obligation to serve two years in an alternate service. The Draft Board still hadn't accepted my request to be recognized as a conscientious objector yet, so it was difficult decision. Finally, my decision was made; I was going to Red Lake anyway, even if it wouldn't satisfy the Draft Board. If my conscientious objector application was rejected, I would deal with it after I spent some time up North.

The next day I drove to Grand Island and went to see the people at the Draft Board office. They still had not ruled in my case, so I informed them that I was going anyway, and that I would come back if things didn't work out. They carefully informed me that I would need to follow their instructions, otherwise the time spent in Red Lake would not count for the time that I was required to serve. I respectfully told them that I wanted to go anyway, and that I would stay in touch with them. Shortly after Christmas 1968 I left for Red Lake, Ontario, to start working with Northern Lights Gospel Mission. I was only in Red Lake a short time when I received my letter from the Draft Board. They recognized my conscientious objector request and approved my service at Northern Light Gospel Mission. I was thankful. It was the beginning of a totally new life.

Betsy's graduation picture, spring of 1968

Everything was new in Red Lake. My room was at the hospitality house with some of the other workers. During the first week there, a young lady from Indiana came through on her way to Poplar Hill Residential School. Her name was Betsy Martin, and after watching her for a bit, I concluded that she would make someone a very good wife. Then I wondered, "Why not me?" She had no such interest or desire for me though, as I still had a lot of the marks of my life before I met Jesus.

I worked along with young men from the eastern States. Many were conservative Mennonites who had been Christians all their lives. The first place I was sent to work was the airplane hangar. Whitey Hostetler had several of the mission planes there and he was rebuilding a Super Cub. The tubular frame needed to be sanded and repaired. My days were spent sanding the tubing. Some days the hangar was full, so I worked outside in the cold. Since it was January, and in northern Ontario, it was cold and snowy. I was often sick from being cold. Somehow I found out that there was a need for more help at Poplar Hill School, so I enquired about it. Shortly after that, I was transferred there and began looking after the generators and keeping all the fires going. This meant that I was up all hours, day and night, so the wood fired stoves would keep going. I also lit the kitchen stove, so it was hot when the cooks came in to start breakfast early in the mornings. I really enjoyed what I was doing. It was fun servicing the generators.

A few months after I started looking after the diesel generators, I was told that one of them needed new rings and bearings. This would be no problem for me as I had rebuilt engines, and of course, in my arrogance, I could do anything. The engine was torn down, cleaned, and all new parts installed. It started perfectly, then came to a screeching halt, a real screeching halt, and would not turn over. The people in charge were not happy with me. The generator was hauled out to Red Lake, and I was removed from the generator responsibilities. My ego was shattered. I had installed one of the crankshaft main bearings wrong, so it didn't get any oil. God was slowly beginning to give me the capacity to change as He broke my arrogant pride. I still looked after the wood stoves but began to do other work as well.

There were difficult, but exciting times at Poplar Hill. I got to know some great, young men who loved the Lord and took their commitment to God very seriously. One of my best friends was John King. His words and actions always matched his intentions, so I knew I could trust him with everything. The more I trusted him, the more I opened up and talked about who I really was, the life I had lived, and also who I wanted to become. I struggled with acceptance because I still saw myself as I had been. One cold night I walked outside and noticed two big spruce trees in the moon light. They were covered in snow. One was crooked leaning off to the left, while one was straight and tall. I identified with the crooked one and felt like I would always be that way. Later that night John King helped me understand that we are all crooked from our birth, since we are born in sin, but God makes us new. Then we become trees of the Lord as we are his plantings. I still think about that when I see some spruce trees all bent over and some right beside them that are straight.

My fondness for Betsy grew, but she still had no feelings for me. It was obvious. At one time she told her brother that John would be the last guy she would date. Actually, this did turn out to be true, and I tease her about it now; but this wasn't what she had in mind. My temper and coarseness was still a problem for me, so the dreaded time came when I realized that I would have to open up to her about who I really was and the life I had lived. I didn't want her to think that I was something I wasn't.

On the night I wrestled with this while trying to go to sleep, she too was troubled because she already knew some things about me. She prayed and told God that if I opened up and told her everything, then she would know that she could trust me, and feel safe in keeping the relationship going. The next day I resolved that I was going to talk to her, not knowing the prayer she had just prayed the night before. I felt pretty certain that once she knew these things about me, she would want to stop the relationship. It would be easier to stop it now than it would be later. So I walked through the kitchen that day while she was cooking, and we just chatted for a bit; then I told her my whole story.

One evening, about a month later, my roommate asked me to go on a double date with him and his fiancé before he left for home. He wanted to go for a boat ride and suggested that

I ask Betsy to go along. I wasn't so sure about it. Finally, after he pressured me for a while, I asked her if she would go along. Much to my surprise she said, "yes." I found out later that she decided she would go but would act real goofy so I would never ask her again. So the big day came and the four of us headed out on the Berens River to fish. Sure enough, Betsy did all kinds of things like dragging the paddle outside the boat, splashing me while I drove the boat, and pinching the gas line so the motor would starve for fuel and die. She was not her normal, very well-behaved self. But this just made me like her even more. Amazingly, our relationship continued, and we grew together in our love for God, and each other. We both knew that God had called us into His service, but we had no idea the path it would be. We would find out as we journeyed.

Since courting was not really encouraged among the single staff at Poplar Hill School, it soon became apparent that it would be best for me to go somewhere else. There was a need at Pikangikum, (puh-CAN-juh-cum) about 50 miles south: I would go and help there. I would live with David and Elva Burkholder and help with the work at that mission station. This was an amazing work of God, for He knew the things I needed to learn from this wonderful family as they served the Lord. I would spend just over a year with them.

I stayed in a bunk house beside their house. I used a kerosene lamp to see in my room at night and used an outhouse for other duties. There were no other young men around, so most of my evenings were spent alone. I read my Bible a lot. Nights were sometimes difficult, especially when I would start remembering the past. The only thing that would stop the troubling memories would be when I got up, lit the lamp, and read my Bible until I fell asleep, exhausted.

The wonderful thing about God's Word is that it washes, and washes, and washes us. The pain of the troubling memories stopped even though I could still remember them. I knew cleanness and freedom from the condemnation because I experienced the washing of His Word, and freedom from sin because of the blood of Jesus from the cross. When you have been bound, freedom is amazing!

I learned a lot of important natural things as well during my time at Pikangikum—important things like hunting, fishing, cutting firewood, and other basic skills need to live in the North. These would be very important just a few short years later.

Moose horns from the first moose I shot at Pikangikum, Ontario

I flew back to Poplar Hill just after Christmas and on January 1, 1970, I asked Betsy if she would marry me. She said yes, but we didn't tell anybody until February 14. People were surprised and some were not very happy with us. Some tried to persuade Betsy that this would not work. Everyone liked her, but they were still not so sure about me. This was understandable. I went back to Poplar Hill to see Betsy several times the next summer. Sometimes I would catch a ride on the mission plane, but other times a friend and I would take a canoe up the river. It was a slow trip as there were some water falls along the way, so we had to carry the boat and motor around on dry land. Our love grew and she stayed firm in her resolve. When school was over, she went back to Indiana. I needed to remain until January 1971 when my required service time would be finished. There were still lessons to learn, changes to be made in my life, and God kept working.

There was a new kind of church movement going on at Pikangikum—a mix of several different church expressions. There was lots of emotion, fervor, and excitement. I heard about it and was interested, so one evening I went to see for myself. As I walked into the room, everyone was standing. The music was loud from the electric guitars playing. I slowly made my way into the room and as I got closer to the front I could hear crying and yelling. It was a very interesting mix, and something felt uncomfortable. When I got to where I could see the front of the room, there were several benches marking off a section in the front corner. There were about ten young children, five to ten years old, dancing around, falling down, and crying most of the time. They looked like they were in very bad pain. I felt compelled to do something for them, so I made my way through the crowd and attempted to get inside the area sectioned off by the benches.

When I got to the benches, an invisible wall would not let me into the area. It felt like I was pushing a thousand pounds aside, and my feet were extremely heavy as I crossed the benches. When I got into the area, the children stopped dancing and falling; they just lay on the floor resting. I began talking about the peace of the gentle wind of the Holy Spirit who was like a dove that John saw when he baptized Jesus. The music got quieter, then stopped. I found myself in a very awkward situation and wanted to disappear. Everyone stared at me wondering why I was there. I encouraged everyone to follow Jesus and I attempted to walk out of the room. It was crowded so I couldn't leave.

The leaders standing up in the front beside where I was, came over and shook my hand. Nobody looked real happy, and I couldn't understand what they were saying as I didn't understand Ojibway. Finally, after what seemed like eternity, I was back outside and walking back to my cabin. For several days I tried to make sense of it all—the music and strange atmosphere, the children falling, looking so painful, yet saying it was worship to God. About a week later I was walking a trail along the lake and I met some of the leaders of that group. They also had some younger men with them who could speak English. They very politely greeted me and spoke about the evening I was at the meeting. They said that I had offended the children since I had stopped the children from worshiping when I walked among them. They told me that Jesus taught that it is better to have a millstone around my neck and drowned in the water than it is to offend the children. I felt very vulnerable standing by the lake and hearing them talk like that! Then they simply shook my hand and went on their way.

I was having to face reality: following the Lord would bring risk, and I could easily make costly mistakes. But I wanted my motivation to be my love for Him and not my own preservation.

I was learning to recognize when God would prompt me to pay attention to Him. Sometimes it was to say something to someone, but at other times it was to do something. Learning to respond to His touch saved my life many times in later years.

CHAPTER 6

Growing Together

1971-1972

The beginning of January 1971 marked the end of my commitment to service at Northern Light Gospel Mission fulfilling my obligation to the Draft Board. I excitedly packed up my stuff in my car, a small Pontiac Tempest, and headed to Indiana. It was so good to see Betsy again and work on our wedding plans scheduled for February 20. I worked for Betsy's brother on the farm milking cows and helping with the farming. Betsy was teaching school, so we were busy as we prepared for our wedding. My folks had moved to Oregon, hoping that it would be easier for mom who was fighting cancer. They were all excited about flying out for the wedding, but shortly before they were to come, Mom got very sick and no one was able to come except my older brother Galen. After all the plans were made and the wedding rehearsal was finished, I went to bed but could not sleep. I was afraid that somehow I wouldn't be able to make a living, pay the bills, take care of Betsy, and raise a family. In spite of my fears, I knew there had to be a way and we would find it. There was so much to learn, and we were about to start an exciting adventure of life, love, and happiness.

Our wedding, February 20, 1971

Several months after the wedding we left Indiana and moved to Oregon to be with my family and help out where we could. I was still driving the Pontiac Tempest which had a four-cylinder engine with a four-barrel carb and a four-speed transmission. We pulled a small U-haul trailer loaded with our stuff. It all went well until we got through Omaha, Nebraska, when all of a sudden, the car wouldn't go any more. I caught a ride to a gas station and called Uncle Robert in Milford. He came to get us and towed us to their place. I think he had a Buick and a long tow rope. He hooked us up and away we went on the Interstate 80. It seemed like we went about 70 miles an hour as I tried to keep from hitting him when he slowed down. When I took it apart, I found that part of the enclosed driveline had broken. Fortunately, we found a used one at some junk yard in Lincoln. Uncle Robert and Aunt Grace blessed us then and many times after that. We made it to Oregon several days later.

All packed up! Leaving Indiana for Oregon

We settled into a small church where Mom and Dad attended. I loved the Lord, and Betsy and I both knew we were called into ministry but couldn't understand where it would be. Our love was still in the North. This was a bit frustrating because there were no openings there. I was hungry to know more of God and to experience the reality of living in His kingdom and to not be so blocked in by this physical world. We were a bit active in the church working with the young people, but not much was happening that we could see. Underneath all this, we were discovering that the safe, externally structured Christianity we had adopted, was not bringing satisfaction or growth in our relationship with our Heavenly Father. I had thought that by embracing this way of living I would have a better chance of not going back to the life that I had before I met the Lord. I would do almost anything if I thought it would keep me from going back. While this lifestyle did give security, it destroyed my adventure of discovering God. A slow wilt began to creep into my spiritual life, and the security of job and potential promotions replaced my peace with God.

Slowly, as we began finding that our way wasn't working, God began to work His plan. We were at a Bible camp one weekend. A speaker, Johnny Stoltzfus, was a missionary that we knew well. One evening after the meeting I shared with him the questions and frustrations I was having. As we stood outside in the dark with only the stars shining around us, he simply put his hand on my shoulder and prayed. He asked for God to lead and show us His plan. I was looking up at the stars as he prayed.

Just as he finished praying, I began to see a very large sheet of paper in the sky. It looked very real even though I knew it was not physical. It looked like the paper had been burned with fire around the edge, and the writing on the page was not in English. As I looked at the writing on the page, I could read and understand it even though I did not recognize the language. Excitement and wonder filled me as I recognized God was talking to me.

A memory returned of my good friend Harold Fly, who was an evangelist and preacher, standing beside me as I fed some cows while we lived in Indiana. About a year earlier, I'd been having some of the same questions. As I stood beside the silo as the chain was taking the silage to the cows, Harold walked over and took off my cap. He placed his hand on my head and began to speak to me in a way I had never heard before. He spoke from the heart of God directly into my soul. The message through Harold Fly and the writing I read were both saying the same thing. God was leading and preparing Betsy and I both for a ministry that God Himself would direct. I was not here to work with physical things but with God for His people. The message also instructed us that we needed to learn to wait and trust. These were very unusual experiences and didn't fit into any of the boxes I had built around God. Somehow I had missed seeing in the Bible that these type of things are very normal activities for God. In the next few months I was going to find out a whole lot more how God works through His Holy Spirit, and the book of Acts would take on new meaning.

Since the routines of life can easily dull the spiritual senses, dullness slowly began again to creep into our lives. A promotion at work, talk of more promotions, and buying a nice car began to give me a different sense of self-worth that was separate from my relationship with God. But since God knows the times and seasons of our lives, He sent a phone call our way at the perfect time. I speak of His perfect time, not mine. The call came to us one evening while we were visiting some friends.

A church in Vanderhoof, British Columbia, was looking for someone to fill the vacancy at the mission outpost at Fort Ware. We had never heard of it, so we knew nothing about it. They only wanted us for six months at this point, but it had the possibility of being extended. Now we really needed to know what God wanted. Was this just another option, another distraction or issue to face? It was really difficult because I had grown to really enjoy my job. Mom was bedridden with cancer, so we spent a fair bit of time with her. She enjoyed her first granddaughter, our daughter Faith. Faith would play on the bed while Mom read to her and enjoyed being a grandma. It would be hard to leave.

That night after going to bed, I could not sleep so I got up and went outside. We lived right beside the church we attended, so I walked over to it, sat on the back steps, and tried to pray. The mosquitoes were so bad that I spent all my time swatting and fighting them. The back door of the church was unlocked, so I went inside and sat on the steps going down to the basement. I talked to God and asked a lot of questions about the whole uncertain situation. The more I tried to understand the situation we were facing, the further away God seemed to get. Finally, I stopped, got quiet, and just waited. Then, in the quietness, I heard God asking me, "John, will you give up your job?" I liked my job, but it wasn't too hard to agree and give it. "What about your car?" He wanted to know if He could take it, too. It was a nice car, but not something that would keep me from God. So after thinking of how God might take it, I agreed. Then God got serious and He said He wanted to have Faith, our daughter who was almost a year old. This was really difficult, and I fought long and hard. I knew that whatever I agreed to give to Him, I could never have again for myself or claim as mine. After crying and struggling with what I thought might happen, I gave up Faith.

Then the last question came; it was the hardest of all. He asked, "Will you let me take Betsy?" All I can remember is the pain of having to give up the closest, most important thing to me in the world. We had been married less than two years, and I didn't see how God could ask something like this of anyone. What was the point of all this questioning? It all seemed so unfair. I knew I was dealing with God Himself, and this was for real. I felt like eternity was watching and waiting. Finally, honestly, without holding on to anything, I was able, by His Grace, to give Betsy to Him. I didn't feel any flood of emotion or relief, but that same strange, warm, secure feeling that I had when I first met the Lord came over me. I knew I had made some agreements with God that related to things invisible. I went to bed and slept.

Next morning that same warm, secure feeling was still there as I got into the car to drive to work. The dealing of the night before was still very fresh and alive. Normally, I would never buckle the seat belt, but this morning I did. I was sure there would be an accident since I had given the car to God. I had said good-bye to Betsy and Faith, feeling like they may be gone by the time I got off work. It seemed so strange to have this safe, secure feeling, while being convinced that God was about to take everything away from me. I was about to discover how little I knew of God's way, and the tender love and care He has for us. I was about to learn that even though we give everything to God, we are never without the blessing of God giving back to us. But one thing is different: we are very conscious that everything belongs to God, and we are secure because of it.

I went off to work; Betsy went to spend the day with Mom. After work I stopped by their house to pick up Betsy and Faith. Betsy had told Mom the whole issue of the call and the questions we had about leaving. When I walked into the bedroom, I was faced with a direct question from Mom. "What are you going to do?" I still hadn't settled it yet, so I said, "I don't know." If she could have gotten out of bed, I have a feeling she would have stood up, stretched to her full height of 4 feet 11 inches, and spoke. But as it was, she just laid there and said, "You know exactly what you need to do. Don't wait around here for me to die. I'd rather have you halfway around the world serving the Lord than sitting here waiting for me to die." I could only nod and agree. Her commitment and spiritual strength went far beyond her physical strength and ability. Finally, the issue was settled; we were moving to a mission outpost and a whole new adventure.

I began getting things arranged at work to have someone replace me. We didn't know how we would get from Woodburn, Oregon, to Vanderhoof, British Columbia, but we knew something would work out. I sold the car and some of our stuff. Other things we packed in boxes and stored at my parents' house. As we were packing, Dad told us that he and Mom wanted to drive us up to Vanderhoof. We didn't see how Mom could make such a trip since it would take two days to get there and two days back. But she was determined to go. We were smart enough to not waste time trying to talk her out of it. The day finally came and off we went. Mom was delighted and never gave any sign of discomfort, although we knew she was suffering a lot with pain because sitting was very hard for her. We arrived in Vanderhoof early in the afternoon and Mom rested. Later we had supper with our host family. We all went to bed after a fun evening, saving our "good-by" until the next morning. As it worked out, that was the last we saw Mom because they got up early the next morning and left. I think that is how she wanted it because parting would have been very difficult for all of us. She went to be with Jesus, the One she loved with all her heart, only a few short months later. She ended her journey, finally healed and at home, while ours was just beginning.

CHAPTER 7

The Village

1972-1973

From Vanderhoof, we made the hour and a half flight into the village on a late September afternoon. The mission house was located a bit away from the rest of the village, so it was fairly quiet. People mostly came because they wanted medicine. I wanted to build relationships so I could share about Jesus. Most were not interested, and my words had no effect. I was learning that words were not enough, and that life could be very difficult. There were three times in the next several months that I should have been killed but wasn't.

After using my Skidoo to help a drunk man haul his groceries to his house, I carried them inside for him. After getting everything inside, he carefully locked the door and turned to me, stating that he was going to kill me. His gun was in the corner of the room with the shells hanging right beside it in a small moose hide pouch. I watched as his hand went to grab the gun, but his hand could only get within about 4 inches of the gun, but never touching it. After watching him make several attempts, I realized I had time to unlock the door and walk out. As I walked to the Skidoo, he followed, threatening me all the way. He attempted to grab me but was deflected and grabbed the Skidoo instead, shaking it violently. This happened three times before he walked off. So I started the machine and drove home.

We had a small tractor to haul things up from the river boat. One day while attempting to drive it up a steep hill the back tire suddenly fell off. The tractor should have rolled over with me on it, but it didn't. Nothing could explain why it stopped, except God.

After the third encounter, which was with a drunk man while walking on the trail, I had to admit that this was more intense and demanding than I had expected. My faith was being tested as I wondered about my ability and commitment to serve the Lord in this environment. My words were having no impact on anyone, and I was starting to feel like it was only a matter of time before something went wrong and I, or my family, would be killed. Most of the issues were related to the color of my skin rather than my testimony for Jesus. I had no desire to give my life just for the color of my skin. I needed answers and I needed them soon. I could see that I had three options. One would be to leave and tell some good missionary stories about how good God was. I could also leave and pretend it was all just a short time of some new experiences but no real impact on anyone's life. But the third option was most intriguing and interested me the most. That option was to find out God's answer to this present distress, find the power to be more than a conqueror, see people freed from the power of sin, and walk in victory experiencing the miraculous presence of Jesus in daily living.

I chose the third option without knowing the journey it would take us on. My conservative way of thinking had caused me to put many boxes around God so everything could be easily explained. It also left me without much dynamic presence of God because I limited God to only the things I could explain. As I wrestled with Paul's teaching regarding the gifts of the Holy Spirit, I realized that my understanding and relationship to the gifts of the Holy Spirit wasn't the problem; it was my relationship to the Holy Spirit himself that was the problem. This relationship would require a whole new surrender to Jesus—and the power of the Holy Spirit that He would send—if I were to live this kind of life. It would be a life where living or dying were no longer factors to be considered when obediently serving the Lord. It sounded like an exciting way to live, so I began a search to find this life. The phrase "Baptism of the Spirit" was uncommon to me and had no place in the boxes I had built, but now I was going to have to find a place in bring it into my life. As the search continued, I became more convinced that it wasn't just another option; it was to be a necessary part of my life, so the search was on until I found it.

My friend and co-worker, Tom Buerge, lived in a village about 60 miles downriver. I had heard that some miraculous things were happening there so I figured that he must know something of this life I was looking for. As it worked out, Betsy and I needed to fly out to renew our visas to stay in Canada, so we had to go to Prince George. Betsy had flown out ahead of me as I was working fighting forest fires. When the fires subsided, I was flown by helicopter to catch another flight from Ingenika (in-juh-NEE-kah). This would require me to stay at Tom's house overnight. My heart was set; I would ask him to pray for me to receive this "Baptism of the Spirit." I didn't know what it was, or how it would feel; I only knew that I needed it.

That evening, as Tom's house was quieting down, I told him of my desire for the Holy Spirit. He had another visitor from Oregon, Joe Kropf, at his house that same evening. Since he was a pastor in the Mennonite church, I wasn't too sure how all this was going to work out, but Joe was as excited about praying for me as Tom was. As they laid their hands on me and prayed, Jesus sent the Holy Spirit just like He said He would, and I was filled with a new Spirit. I was so overjoyed; I began speaking and praising in another language. I began to see a vision. It was like a dream, except I was awake, which was so much like some other times when I had encountered God while searching for direction in life. This was not an emotional experience; it was the most solid, real, encounter with God that I had ever had. My heart was joined together with these men in a whole new way. We really were brothers. Over 20 years later, when Betsy and I were visiting a church in Brownsville, Oregon, a man turned to us at the end of the service and welcomed us with a big smile. It was Joe Kropf and his wife. He told us that since the time we met, he and his wife had prayed for us daily. Our hearts were joined again.

So after this encounter, my question was, "How different will my life and experience be from what it was before?" I didn't have long to wait. We arrived back in the village very shortly after this. A day or so later I was sitting on our old sofa reading. Three young men walked in and we started talking. Things happened so fast, I'm not real sure how it all happened, but suddenly I realized that these three young men were lying on the floor asking God to forgive them and make them new. When they got up from the floor, the first thing they stated was that we are all brothers now.

I had never talked to them about this. I couldn't figure out what I had said or done to make this happen. I wanted to try and recapture the moment so I could do this again. But I heard the Spirit gently talk to me and teach me that this was His work, not mine. I only needed to be available and stay out of the way so He could do His work. I was to see this happen over and over in the following years. God's simplest way was always more dynamic and effective than the most polished, disciplined ways of man.

CHAPTER 8

Led by The Spirit

1973-1975

L ife was exciting as we daily looked forward to the Spirit leading us. Many times we didn't have a clue, but God was always working. As we began to experience God, many of our beliefs were challenged. I had limited God to a set of boxes without being aware of it, until I watched God do things that didn't match my expectations of Him. He was always so much more!

God's protection over us and our children was amazing. The first spring we were there, Duncan Pierre, a respected elder in the village, walked with me across the river to my wood pile to get my chain saw and check to see if I cut enough wood for the year. We didn't realize that Faith, our oldest daughter who was about two years old, had followed us out the door. As we turned to walk back, we spotted her walking down to the river's edge. She wasn't following the trail but began walking on the ice, straight towards an open area of water. We hollered for her to stop but she couldn't hear us. We ran as fast as we could. Duncan ran the trail while I tried to cut across through the snow. He was faster on the trail and got there first. Just as the ice broke under her feet and she splashed into the water, Duncan was there to grab her before the river current could wash her downriver under the ice. Everything was wet except for a small area on top of the hood of her coat. God used Duncan to save her life.

Our family of four

We went to Eight-mile Cabin to get meat one winter. I borrowed a snow machine since the old one the mission had wasn't very dependable. We loaded up and headed home. The one I borrowed was almost new, so everyone headed out in front and I came last to help anyone who might break down. It was about -40° with a bit of a breeze and it was cold. I hadn't gone very far when the engine on my machine screeched to a halt. The belt on the fan had broken so the engine overheated and seized tight. I left the meat and my backpack and started walking.

I was dressed in insulated coveralls and very warm mitts and hat. Darkness was coming so I needed to hurry as I was still about six miles from home. I walked fast and soon was sweating, causing my clothes to become damp. This was bad as the cold began to creep through my damp clothes. I got very cold and as darkness fell, I also got very tired. I kept walking but my eyes kept closing from being so tired. With my moccasins on, I could feel the edge of the trail since the snow was about a foot above the packed trail. Sometimes I stumbled but somehow always kept going. I had no idea that I was freezing. I only wanted to stop. Then I came on a steep bank in the trail. As I half slid and half fell down the bank, I realized that I was only one mile from home. It woke me up. With strength and awareness that only God could give, I walked the last mile to our house. It was pitch dark and the light from the window was very bright. I opened the door, walked to the kitchen table, and sat down. Faith noticed that I had come in but didn't recognize me, so she just said, "Mom, somebody came in." Home is a wonderful place!

God did some wonderful things there. I worked hard and always wanted to be involved in the activities of the village. One day several of us were standing along the riverbank, and one of the older men stopped by to see if anyone wanted to go hunting with him. He asked the two men on my right if they would go with him. They both said no. He skipped me and asked the ones on my left if they would go. The all said no. Then he looked at me and with a frown asked, "You?" I could tell he was pretty desperate for someone to go and wasn't really excited about having me. I was so excited as I had really been working to get to know this man.

I ran home, packed a few things, got my gun, and off we went downriver. After going downriver several miles, we stopped at a place we called "Hole in the Wall." It was along a big cut bank where a small creek flowed into the Finlay. We walked upstream for a while, tried moose calling, and waited, hoping for moose to show up. It was fairly windy, and nothing showed up. As we were walking back to the boat a spruce grouse flew up and landed on the top of a tall spruce tree. It was moving back and forth in the wind. We stopped and he said, "Shoot it, I want to eat it." I looked at my 30-06 rifle with open sights, then up at the bird swaying almost directly above us. I raised the rifle to my shoulder, tried to hold the sight on the bird, and prayed for a perfect shot so I could hit it without blowing it to pieces. I pulled the trigger expecting to see an explosion of bird and feathers come raining down on us. The bird just dropped straight down in one piece. The bullet went right through his neck, but the head was still attached by a small piece of skin. He simply said, "Gee, good shot." I was thinking, "Dear God, what a miracle!" After this we had many more hunting trips, and I drank lots of tea at his house. A few short years later he helped me build my boat and did lots of work helping us build our house. He was a great man and I enjoyed being around him.

During this time, several people in the village were contracting tuberculosis and were being sent to Vancouver to the sanitarium. We had lots of contact with everyone in the village, often drinking tea and eating at other people's houses. We thought nothing of it. But as TB became a serious issue, the health nurses came in to check everyone. Then I began to have some unpleasant health problems, a bit of cough, waking up at night with sweating, and shortness of breath at times during the day. Then one day while walking, I started coughing and spit out some blood. I was not happy.

The nurses were doing their routine testing again and gave me the shot in my forearm to check for a reaction. It was a very big reaction and it was obvious that my body had lots of TB antibodies. Then they wanted to do chest x-rays. I couldn't imagine being sent to Vancouver and getting stuck in a hospital. There was too much to do. So I got word out to several people to pray specifically for healing from TB. I avoided the x-ray people when they came in to test people. Slowly, my cough went away, the night sweats stopped, and I got my energy back. God had healed me.

God began moving in the village, people were giving their hearts to God and believing and praying. It became normal to pray when someone was sick and then see them recover. We were far from medical help so when one got hurt or very sick the only option was prayer. I watched some young men pray for a very sick baby with lips turning blue and unable to breath, but as they prayed, the baby started breathing normally and good color came back to the lips. These young believers were never surprised, but I was continually amazed.

I returned to the village one afternoon after being gone a few days. I stopped in to see an old couple whose cabin was close to ours. The old grandpa had been sick in bed, his legs too weak to hold him up. Everyone was concerned for him and was praying for him. When I walked in, he was sitting up on the edge of the bed and very excited to see me. He began to thank me for coming into his house the night before. I tried to explain to him that I was gone last night and had just gotten back in the village a few hours ago. But he wouldn't listen to me. He kept thanking me for coming in during the night and praying for him. He insisted that during the night when he needed to go to the bathroom, that I had come in, laid my hands on his legs, and prayed. Then he said that I told him, "Get up." So he did and was now walking around. My mind swirled as I tried to make sense of what happened. I can only assume that sometimes God makes his angels look like people, so they are welcomed and trusted. That old grandpa called me his grandchild for many years.

One summer while coming upriver with a load of freight for us, my outboard motor began running very poorly. Since I was loaded and going upstream, my progress was very, very slow. I was about 12 miles downriver and wondering if I would even make it. All I could do was hope and pray to God that the engine wouldn't stop completely, and that I would get home before dark. I came around a bend in the river and spotted a helicopter sitting on an island in the middle of the river. As I made my way towards him, I decided to stop and let the outboard cool off. The pilot watched me slowly approach and beach the boat. He walked over and commented about how slow I was going. I explained that the outboard was not running very well. He told me he had gotten tired and stopped for a rest. Then he told me to jump into the helicopter and he would take me to the village to get another outboard. A short time later I was back on the river with a good outboard pushing me and my load home. The impulses of the Holy Spirit are amazing and perfectly timed!

I was driving the boat up to the house one afternoon. Someone on the bank was waving me to come to shore, so I pulled in. He jumped into the boat and told me to take him upriver. He was very angry and ready to kill his brother-in-law because of a big fight they had. He told me to take him upriver so he could get away before he actually went through with it. We headed upriver to a cabin about eight miles away. We had only gone about 200 yards when he told me to pull over. He said that there was no use to go upriver, but that he might as well do it and get it over with. As he jumped out of the boat and started up the bank, I called out and said, "When you get home he will be there and tell you he wants to be friends." He took off for his house while I sat in the boat wondering why I would say something like that. Several days later he came to the house and still in shock said, "It was exactly like you said." I was as surprised as he was. The Holy Spirit moves beyond our understanding and speaks of things before they happen.

As these kind of things kept happening, word reached our mission board. They were happy about people getting saved and learning to pray, but our experiences with the Holy Spirit didn't match the teachings of the church that we worked with, so it was judged as a false expression. After many discussions about these things, we were asked to meet with the conference mission board in Oregon.

By this time there were all kinds of rumors going around about the things we were teaching. Most were greatly exaggerated and simply false. We were accused of very strange things. One statement we had to deal with was that I supposedly taught that a man could have two wives—one he called his "natural" wife and the other his "spiritual" wife. I was told that I had Betsy as my natural wife and one of the native women in the village was my spiritual wife. I could never figure out how things can get so twisted and far from the truth. But God knew and had a plan.

As we sat and talked with the board in Oregon, they presented a list of about eight things that addressed the false doctrines that I was supposedly teaching. None of them were even close to accurate, so we talked a long time to try to understand from where these things came. At the end of our discussion, we all agreed that these statements did not at all represent what I was teaching.

The next day while I was with my dad, one of the board members that was present during the discussion brought the list of statements and asked me to sign it. I didn't want to sign it because it did not represent what I believed and taught. I was told that no one would see this list except the board members. The signature was only to show that we talked about these subjects, not that I believed those exact statements. I signed it with great reluctance. The conclusion reached was that we needed to go to Bible School so we could get our doctrines straightened out. I would have loved to go but with so much happening in the village, I didn't see any way that I could leave for several months. We agreed to wait six months and meet again.

We flew back to the village excited at all that God was doing and forgot about all the discussions about doctrines. We knew we had six months before we would confront the subject again. However, it wasn't to be. The mail came to the village once a month and with the mail came some surprises. As we started to read our mail, one letter came from the local church that supported us in British Colombia. In the letter they stated that they were hurt and saddened when they heard the announcement in church that Sunday stating that the mission board was no longer supporting us due to our doctrines. We were surprised and thought they must have misunderstood because we were to visit this issue in six months.

We opened another letter; it read the same. Finally, we decided the only way we would know if we were still being supported was to check our bank statement. We checked and there was no deposit from the mission. So we discovered the support had stopped without any official notification from the mission. Then another letter from a church in Nebraska stated that they were saddened to read a list of things that we believed. This list had been posted on the bulletin board in their church, and they would not have believed it, but my signature was on the bottom. This was the same list that I had signed while with Dad in Oregon.

I was sad to learn that in spite of the promise that this was a private list, to only show the things we discussed and no one else would see it, it had been mailed out to churches that had supported use and used to stop all support. I couldn't blame them for not supporting us. If I was told someone believed the things on that list, I would stop supporting them too. With great disappointment we started preparing for an unknown future, all the while knowing that God had a plan and would care for us. We would need a house to live in, but even more than that, we needed a place for a house and food for the winter.

Things began to open soon enough. The village chief and council talked things over and stated that they wanted us to stay. They chose a spot for our house in the middle of the village. Some of the guys would help me build a cabin. Now there were so many things to be done and no money to do it. A year's supply of groceries had to be gotten, shipped up the lake, and then hauled the 60 miles up the Finlay River. We didn't know how, but God did.

Our log house at Ft. Ware, B.C. The dog
sled is on top of the woodshed.

Soon we got a message that a friend of ours, Jack Wright, from Edmonton, was flying in to see us. After landing his plane on our dirt airstrip, he walked down to the house with us. He told us he had gotten a message from a church in Miami, Florida. They had somehow heard of us and wanted to support us. They told him to fly in to see us and bring us a bunch of cash. I think there was about $500 in the roll that he handed to me. Another church from Edmonton sent us windows and a wood cook stove. Other people offered to come in and help cut logs, some offered to build cabinets. Don and Dorothy Rutherford came. He helped me peel logs for the cabin. We built a friendship that lasted until they went to be with the Lord. One of the men from the village offered to help me build the cabin and do all the log corners. He did a very nice job and the cabin was very warm. By the time fall arrived, the house was built, food bought and hauled upriver, and we were settled into our new house. Over $2, 000 had come in to help. Some came in the mail, some was handed to us directly, but we knew that it had all come as people were led by the Holy Spirit to help us in our journey.

CHAPTER 9

More Adventure

(1975-1978)

L ife can become very routine if you let it. There was always wood to cut and split since we cooked and heated the house with wood. Water always needed to be carried up from the river; then it was used and carried back outside and dumped. Money was always needed to buy food and clothes, so I would take jobs whenever there was work available. I worked fighting forest fires, drove river boats to haul freight, and sometimes worked for an outfitter taking nonresident hunters out looking for moose, black bear, grizzly bear, caribou, mountain goats, or fishing. There were times I would be gone for weeks at a time. God always had a provision. It was always hard leaving Betsy home alone with the three little ones. She went through some very difficult trials during those times, but God always kept her safe, and we always had what we needed.

Hitching up the dogs to haul firewood

One year we felt the need to go back to Indiana to visit Betsy's family. With no car, no money, and three children, we trusted that God would have a plan to take care of the details. As it turned out, Dad offered us the use of his car and came to Fort St. John to pick us up. We had friends and family all along the route from British Colombia to Oregon, to Indiana, back to Oregon, and then home. We had very little cash for going to Oregon, when we met some people on the road as we were heading for the Alaska Highway. They stopped us and told us they had a check they wanted to give us. It was several hundred dollars. We thought that MIGHT be enough to pay for our gas, and knew we would need to be very careful so we would have enough to get back home.

When we got to Oregon, my brother handed me his credit card and insisted that I use it to buy all the gas for the trip. I was amazed how this was all working out. As we traveled I often thought about what I would do when we got back home because I needed a boat and outboard motor. The motor would be almost $800, which was a lot of money for us. We had a wonderful time with family and friends and also spoke in several small church groups that had heard about us and wanted to hear what was happening in the North. Every church took an offering to help us with our work.

We arrived back home in the village, and I counted how much money we had. It was $800! I ordered the outboard motor. Then I got to work falling trees with my chainsaw to build a river boat. I ripped logs into one-inch-thick boards and stacked them to dry. I couldn't afford plywood, but I had seen some of the other boats and felt like I could make a copy of one with boards. My good friend, John McCook, had one by his house and he offered to help me with mine.

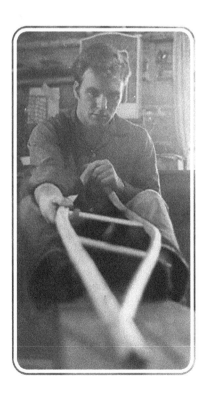

Making a new set of snowshoes

After the boards had dried enough, I got my hand saw and began ripping them into boards the proper width. It was a lot of work; days were spent ripping these boards by hand. I spent one whole month building the river boat measuring 26 feet long with a 36-inch bottom. The new motor had arrived and was set on the new boat transom. It ran perfectly and the boat worked exceptionally well on the Finlay river as well as the Kwadacha (also known as the White River) and Wolverine Rivers. While the Finlay was wide and easy, the other two were narrow and shallow and could be difficult to navigate.

In the spring after breakup, we often had to cut our way through log jams to get our boats upriver. One year I had the family in the boat and was trying to cut logs out of the way when a log came loose and slammed the boat sideways sending it and everyone in it, right onto a sand bar. It took a bit of work to get us back into the river. Thankfully, no one was hurt, and no damage done to the boat. Another time we found a log blocking the river as we went down stream. I had the family all get to the back of the boat so the front could be higher and go over it. As the outboard pushed the boat up on the log, everyone slowly went to the front. This caused the front to go down and the back of the boat came up and slid across the log. It was an excellent river boat.

We began spending more and more time up the White River with other families. We found some places where the "old timers" had planted gardens, and we wanted to start growing things again. Rhubarb grew with stalks six feet long from the ground to the end of the leaves. The soil was so rich. There was also good hunting, fishing, and trapping at the forks about 18 miles upriver. There was a cabin at the forks to stay in, but when we brought our families, we pitched tents, and cooked outside. Betsy did a good job of taking care of our family in all these challenging conditions. There was always brush to clear away from the tent, fire to keep going for cooking food or a quick cup of tea, water to be carried from the river, clothes to be washed, and all the time watching the children.

On one of our times camping at the forks, I had gone with the other men upriver to hunt. Betsy was with the children and other families at camp. At that time, our fourth child, Jewel, was just a several months old baby. As Betsy was busy around the tent, one of the other ladies shouted out, "Nathan is in the river!" Somehow he had walked just upstream from camp and gotten in the river. The river was a very cold glacier stream and very milky in color. All Betsy could see was the top of his hood as she spotted him floating downstream past camp.

She started quickly walking out into the river, hoping it was not too deep. There was a log jam just down from camp and she did not want to let him get past her, so with her eyes fixed on him, she hurried out to catch him. The water was chest deep and getting deeper as she got to him. Finally, she was able to grab hold of him, put him under her arm, and make her way back to shore. By the time she got there he was coughing and breathing again. She quickly got into a sleeping bag with Nathan to warm him up. That night we had a long serious talk about what we were doing and how we wanted to raise our family. But most importantly, was God starting to show us that our time there was coming to a close? It was a very difficult question to face.

Through it all, God's grace was very evident. We got a letter in the mail from our good friend Eli Miller shortly after this happened. It was written the same day that Nathan fell in the water. But even more specific, he said he had a burden to pray for us that day. As he closed the letter he stated that it was 6:00 and he was going to supper. He was in a different time zone than us. It was 5:00 where we were—the exact time that Betsy was getting Nathan out of the water. It is an honor to have friends that pray when God impresses it on them.

Shortly after this we experienced some other difficult situations and wondered again what God was wanting us to do. I had felt so firmly that living and ministering here in the village was my calling, and that I would see a strong, growing church that loved and served the Lord. The difficulties we experienced would pass, and I would again focus on what I felt was God's work for me.

One winter we had gone to a church convention with a lot of visiting ministries. We respected these leaders and often communicated during these times. After one of the meetings, several of us were talking together and I was asked to share what was happening in our lives at the village. At that time, I couldn't think of anything positive or encouraging to say, even though I wanted to give some sort of a good report. Finally, I opened up, shared all the difficulties we were experiencing, and related how God had met us and carried us through. Our greatest concern was for our family as our children were growing with the oldest almost seven years old. One of the men, Brother Sam, looked at me and said, "You're a fool to stay there, it's time to come out."

He had visited us a year or so earlier and after walking down to our cabin from the airstrip, simply stated, "You live in a snake pit." We had simply shrugged his words off by feeling like he didn't understand our situation at that time. Now it was different. I couldn't talk about leaving; it was too difficult. During the meetings there were a lot of different people speaking, but one line kept coming from Brother Sam regarding what the Bible says about "the circumcising of the heart." I couldn't follow along with it very much, as my greatest concern was, "How could I be faithful to the work I felt called to, and be faithful to my family at the same time?" I still felt like I would probably live all my life in the village as I couldn't imagine any other place of ministry that God might have for me.

At the end of the church convention, I was asked to go along to the conventions in Alaska. I would be flying with several others and be gone about two weeks. I thought this would be interesting, so I went. Once again I listened to several hours of preaching and teaching regarding the circumcision of the heart. It meant nothing to me. But one thing was still bothering me; Why would Brother Sam say that we were fools to stay at the village? How could any man with faith leave just because there were tough times? My chance to ask him came one evening as we were visiting in the living room of some friends' house. I moved to a chair right beside him and asked, "How can you say that we are fools to stay where we are? I believe God impressed on me that I would see a strong, faithful, growing church." His response was direct from God. He said, "Johnny, (he was one of only two people that I allowed to call me that), we could get the strongest elders we have, or the strongest apostolic ministries we have, and get them to move in with you to help you, and it wouldn't change anything. But I guarantee you, if you come out of there and let God circumcise your heart, and I let God circumcise my heart, one day we will return and we will see a nation born in a day" (Isaiah 66:8). In that moment I understood that the work God wanted to do "in" me was of far greater significance than the work He wanted to do "through" me. Now I understood the truth about the circumcision of the heart, and I could see that this was not going to be easy.

Returning back home, the village life continued. I was still trying to process all that I was learning and trying to figure what God really wanted us to do. One night I had a strange dream. I dreamed that there were three fighter jets, like bombers, circling overhead. Then a loudspeaker from one of the planes announced, "This is a trial pass," and flew down low over us as if he was landing and pulled back up again. Then another message came over the speaker saying, "This is the test drop," and as the second plane came in low it dropped a dummy bomb that hit the ground and bounced. In the dream I just casually watched it all happen, until the message came very loud over the speaker from the third plane. It was my father's voice, **"John, why are you still here?"** I woke up shaking. I knew God was getting my attention.

Betsy and I talked more about what we should do, but did nothing until it was forced on us. Fall came and I was going to work for the outfitter guiding big game hunters. I was usually gone about two months, but it was a good source of income, and I got to spend a lot of time in the bush with other men. One afternoon, Rick, the owner of the company, flew into camp and told me to pack my bags. He was taking me home and would bring me back after I had my family safely out of the village.

He had been in the village the night before and some very bad things had happened to the four Catholic nuns who ran the school. His conclusion was that it was no longer safe to leave my family there alone. The decision for us to leave was made by someone else, but we agreed it was best. When I arrived home, Betsy and I talked about what to do, where to go, and how do we get out? We called a very good friend, Brother Dee, who was a pilot and had flown in and out with us a few times. He agreed to come and pick up Betsy and the four children and take them to a Christian community, Graham River Farm, that was willing to take us in until we could sort out what and where God wanted us. After packing up what she could take in the small plane, they were gone. I would finish packing and go back to work until the end of hunting season. Then I would fly out on a scheduled flight with some more stuff and catch a bus to Fort St. John. Later our good friend Jim Buerge flew me back in with his plane for a last load of our stuff. Jim and I loaded our stuff in the plane and took off from the airstrip. Jim circled the village once, then flew down the river in front of the village. I looked out the window through eyes filled with tears, and six years of wonder flooded my memory. I looked away, sobbing like a baby, as Jim turned the plane and headed east over the mountains. It hurt so bad to leave and have no idea about the future. If we could have seen God at that time, we would have, like Moses, seen His back side, because He had already gone before us and was leading the way.

CHAPTER 10

Moving Beyond

(1978-1986)

We settled into Graham River Farm and for a while enjoyed the quietness and security of living close to other believers. Our children were doing well in school. One day we discovered that our children were also feeling the quietness and security as six-year-old Steve said to Nathan who was 5, "We don't have to be afraid here, we're safe."

The pull to go back to Fort Ware was still very strong, and we wondered if we might go back but move upriver instead of living in the village. So in the spring of 1980, Bill Ritchie and I flew in to go beaver trapping up the White River with some of the local trappers. After flying our stuff in and loading the boat, we headed upriver 18 miles to the forks. Our plan was to go a few miles beyond the forks and cut logs for a cabin. We planned on returning later that summer to build the cabin and possibly move in yet that fall. It was early spring, so the water was still fairly low with no log jams. Once we arrived at the forks, we unloaded our boat and settled into our tent.

We would trap beaver that evening and go farther upriver tomorrow. However, the next day when we attempted to go upriver, we found a very large log jam with ice frozen all through it. The river was blocked. We weren't too concerned as we had seen that before and were often amazed how quickly it can thaw and open up. We continued trapping mornings and evenings, while our days were spent looking at the log jam and wondering how soon it would open.

About 10 days later we realized that we couldn't just stay there and trap because we were burning up fuel in the outboard, and we wouldn't have enough to get upriver and back down again. Next morning as Bill and I made breakfast over the fire, he said, "John, it's over. We need to go back and forget about this whole plan." I was shocked at his statement and not very happy about how he felt. I had known Bill for a long time and knew he was not a quitter. Difficulties never stopped him, so I was very surprised when he would not change his mind as I tried to convince him that we could just go back down to the village and get more gas.

I decided that I needed to go for a long walk by myself. I picked up my 22-cal. rifle and walked upriver to the log jam. It was as solid as ever, impossible to get through. I started up the mountain hoping to find some blue grouse to shoot and bring home for supper. I walked and walked, higher and higher, losing all track of time. Clouds came in and it started to rain so I crawled in under a big spruce tree to stay dry. I sat there feeling sorry for myself and wishing Bill could change his mind. I was ready to send him home and do it alone. The clouds got heavier, just like my heart, and the rain continued, so I stayed under the spruce tree. After a long time passed, I was able to let go and ask God what He wanted. Clearly, I heard these words in my heart, "Let it go; it's over." The rain soon stopped, and I began the long walk back to camp. I had been gone all day, but Bill was still at camp waiting for me.

We talked again, but this time I agreed with him. The next morning, we packed up and headed back down river. This time it was really over.

Outside our cabin at Graham River Farm near Ft. St. John, B.C.

The time at Graham River was a good time. I taught some math classes in the high school, worked in the shop, milked cows, and helped with haying. But all the time I knew this was a temporary step. Eli Miller would often challenge me to not get comfortable but to keep searching to see where God wanted our family to serve the Lord. When he would talk, I often thought of a place I had visited just outside of Dawson City, Yukon. It was a pretty rustic place with cold, hard winters and a small church community going through lots of changes. We decided to go, but to first make a trip back to Indiana and Oregon to visit family.

We didn't have a vehicle, so I began looking for one. I found a 1967 Dodge Fargo van in Prince George. I went to look at it because it was the only vehicle that I had enough money to buy. It was tired with lots of miles and lots of rust along the bottom panels. It would do and I bought it. It was an open van so I built seats and a bed in the back where the children could sleep while we drove. It was a good trip, and everyone treated us royally. The most common question from the children at mealtime was, "Is this moose meat?" If the answer was no, they didn't want it. They didn't like beef, chicken, turkey, hot dogs, or pork. They only wanted some moose meat and couldn't understand why nobody had any. However, we always enjoyed the ice cream! I think it is a genetic thing.

Our move finally came, and in the fall of 1980, after having shipped our things north, we packed ourselves into the van and started the 1900-kilometer (about 1200 miles) journey north to Rock Creek, Yukon Territory. The children were all very tired of traveling and were not wanting to get in or out of the van by the time we arrived late one afternoon. The cabins were cold and rustic, but the people were warm and friendly. Winter was just ready to set in by the time we arrived and unpacked all our stuff.

Our Dodge Fargo van loaded up and ready for
the move to the Yukon, fall of 1980.

We were to learn a lot about the cold that winter. It would get down and stay between -40F and -60F for six weeks (except for one day). It was cold and we burned a lot of firewood just to keep the houses and the people in them from freezing. I found that at -40° the front wheels on the Fargo van would not roll. The wheel bearing grease was like a rock, so I had to remove it and put regular gun grease in the wheel bearings. The tires would get flat spots from setting and would thump down the road for a long way before they would round out again.

Nathan, wearing a cap, and Steve checking rabbit snares at -40°.

When spring finally came, we had huge amounts of ice buildup on the roof of our two-story cabin. I didn't want it to slide off and hit anyone, so I got a ladder and went to work. The ice was frozen solid to the roof, but if I hit it with a sledgehammer it would slide off in pieces. I thought the easiest thing to do would be to get up on the roof and knock off the ice as I worked my way back to the ladder. I stepped out on the roof ice and started chipping away when the whole sheet let go. I slid down the roof joining the large chunks of ice in a pile on the hard-packed snow beside the house. I landed on my side but didn't get hurt. I noticed a little boy, John Buerge, about six years old, had watched it all happen. I got up and tried to act like nothing had gone wrong. The next day I decided to try again but to just stay on the ladder and work. I was about halfway up when I looked down and there was John Buerge again, watching. He said, "I want to watch you fall again." He did not get to see me fall this time, as I was very careful.

There was another big fall while we lived in that house. There was a railing at the top of the stairs to keep people from falling down. But somehow our son Nathan fell through and went all the way to the bottom, very badly breaking his right arm. We rushed him in to the doctor in Dawson City. The doctor wanted me to hold Nathan on my lap while he pulled to set the bone in position before casting it. He must have known it was going to be painful, so he sent Betsy out to wait in the hall. I did not like how this was looking. Nathan cried really hard as the doctor pulled and twisted on his arm. So the doctor gave him a shot in his arm at the location it was broken and started pulling again, while I tried to hold Nathan and his arm back. Suddenly, I started to see large black dots coming at my eyes, and they got very big as I started getting very weak and light-headed. I told the doctor, "I think we better get Betsy in here." So Betsy came in while I sat in the hall with my head down trying to get the big black dots to stop coming at me. Finally, Nathan had his cast on, and the big black dots stopped coming at me.

We did salmon fishing on the Yukon River one summer. Several of us set up tents at Caribou Creek and lived there about a month. We set nets and checked them twice a day. It was so much fun working with Mark Kearn and his family. We didn't pay too much attention to wildlife but were careful not to leave food laying out. After we would cut up the fish, the ladies would can them in jars. All the scraps went into the river, so our camp was very clean. Our tents were small, so we set up another very small pup tent right outside our front door where Faith and her friend slept. One night her friend had gone home for a few days, so Faith was alone in the tent. Sometime around 4 a.m. we heard her call, so Betsy jumped up and opened the tent door. A black bear was right there and had just flattened the tent on top of Faith. Immediately Betsy said, "There's a bear," so I crawled out of my sleeping bag, grabbed my rifle, and ran outside only in my shorts. I hollered for Mark and he joined me with his rifle as well. We spotted the bear and got a few shots at him, but it was too dark to really see our sights, and the bear got away. We sat up for a long time hoping he would return, but he didn't so we went back to bed. When we got up for breakfast, it looked like the bear had returned and left his muddy paw prints on the table and around the cook stove. We remained alert for him.

Fish camp at Caribou Creek on the Yukon River. Our tent and the smaller one that got flattened by the bear.

Cleaning King salmon at fish camp on the Yukon River

Several days after this, Nathan and I were going out to check nets early in the morning. We walked down to the boat, and when we got there a black bear jumped out of the boat and stood up to us about thirty feet away. Nathan crawled up on my shoulders while the bear rocked back and forth popping his teeth at us. It was obvious that he was afraid of us and didn't want us any closer. We felt the same way. As we both just stood there, I think we looked pretty big with me holding Nathan on my shoulders. Finally, he went down on all four legs and ran the other direction. We were happy and thankful.

There were several small groups living at different isolated locations in the Yukon. As we got to know everyone, we quickly identified with them since we too had lived some years in isolation. At one time there was a need to help at Maisy Mae Creek on the Stewart River, as a family needed to come out for the winter. So we moved. Moving with a river boat was an interesting trip. It reminded us of our time on the Finlay River. Maisy Mae was a beautiful spot on the North side of the river. We used horses to cut and haul in the hay which fed the cows and goats. There was very good moose hunting in the area as well. We always had plenty of meat and vegetables from the garden.

One fall I was moose hunting by myself. I had gone upriver about a mile on the opposite side of the river. There had been moose tracks along the shore, so I hoped to call in something. I walked in about half a mile from the river and found a bit of a hill, so I went to the top and started to call. I could see a pretty good area and sat down and called several more times. Instead of a moose coming out of the bush, a very large grizzly bear appeared about a hundred yards away. I had a tag for him, but I was only using a 30-30 rifle with open sights and didn't trust myself at that distance with such a small rifle. It soon became apparent that he had heard me calling and was interested in finding me, thinking that I was an animal for him to kill and eat. He headed towards me but was going more to the left side moving very quickly. I waited for him to get closer and fired a shot. This made him really speed up. Circling around, he ran right in front of me while I was trying to get another shell in the chamber. As he circled out around again, about a hundred yards away, I fired another shot broad side, hitting him just above the shoulder and breaking his back. He dropped. I ran back to the boat and went to Maisy May to get a couple other men with larger rifles before going to check on the condition of the bear. When we arrived back and found him, he had died on the spot. We skinned him out and found he was a very large, old, bear. I was proud of my 30-30 but never took it hunting again when I was by myself. I got a 7mm magnum and felt much safer after that.

We moved back to Rock Creek after spending two winters and a summer at Maisy May. As we settled back again, I was impressed with a desire to start a business that could make enough money to support a family and give us the ability buy an airplane that we could use to support the outposts. I would also need to learn to fly. This would take thousands of dollars which I didn't have. I had worked at the Demptser Corner for the MacGillivrays doing mechanic work for quite some time and really enjoyed being with them. Don and Joyce, the parents, and Lewis and Diane, their son and his wife, have been very good friends of ours for many years now. It was hard to leave that job, fix up an old shop close to our house, and start up on my own.

Shortly after I started the business, the property where we lived was being put up for sale. I needed to find another place. God was working to get everything together. I was good friends with the pastor of the Pentecostal church in Dawson City, and he had a guest speaker who was very alive in his relationship with the Lord. So we had him come and speak at our church. His message was on the personal care that God has for us. He made it very clear that God knows our needs and moves to supply all our needs. He suddenly stopped and declared that someone here has their toes crossed and it's painful. He wanted to show that God cares, so he would pray and ask God to uncross these toes. No one moved for prayer until our son, Steve, raised his hand. We were aware that he had two toes crossed and at times complained about them hurting him. Steven went up for prayer and God uncrossed his toes. The sermon about this personal God continued until he stopped and said that someone here is needing an airplane and that God was ready to give it. There were quite a few people there, so I didn't want to jump up. But no one spoke up, so finally, I told him that it was me. He prayed for me and asked God for the airplane. As he prayed I saw a small airplane, blue and yellow, which is odd colors for an airplane. He finished praying and as I walked back to my seat he said, "Oh, if you see a vision of what you are asking for in color, it often means that it is close." I couldn't figure out how he knew that but found it interesting to ponder.

During the spring and summer of 1985 we looked around for a place to move and start a repair business. We looked at property in Mayo but found nothing. Then someone told us of a gas station at Stewart Crossing that had been offered for lease. With instructions from Ray Held, our friend and accountant, we went to Stewart Crossing to look it over. After getting all the information that Ray wanted, we returned home. I showed everything to Ray. After several minutes of pounding his calculator, he looked at me grinning and said, "You will make good money there."

That summer we secured the lease but had no place to stay, so we looked for a mobile home that we could set up there. We found one in Faro, (several hours away) and it was a good price. We had no money but got private financing to secure it. By September first we had the house set up, we were moved in, and I took over the gas station and shop. I was hoping for lots of repair work. The gas station was open seven days a week, 7 a.m. to 10 p.m. and I was running it alone. The house was small, so the only office space was in our bedroom. It wasn't long until I was worn out and our money was all spent on inventory. A major problem faced us: we needed several thousand dollars to buy more fuel. We didn't have it and couldn't get any more. It looked like we were finished, tired, and broke. That day the sales rep from White Pass (a fuel wholesale company) called and asked if we needed anything. I told him we needed gas but didn't have any money. He came up from Whitehorse and we worked out a deal where they would fund us a load at a time until summer when we would catch up. Now we were only tired and broke, just not finished. I could not keep the schedule of working all day and doing paperwork at night in the bedroom, so I called a good friend of mine, Don Lefler, who was living in Fort Nelson at the time. I offered him a partnership position if he would come and join me and he agreed. His son Jason came and worked until Don and his wife JoAnn could move up and start working.

The business did well the first year. One day in the spring of 1987, a friend from Mayo walked in and offered me his airplane for eighteen thousand dollars if I would pay half now and the balance in 6 months. I went to look at it and noticed it was blue and yellow. I didn't have the money, but someone had previously offered to finance a plane if we needed help. Wow! A 1946 Taylorcraft BC12D complete with floats and a 90 horsepower Continental engine was ours to start using in God's work in the Yukon. I had just started flying lessons and had recently soloed, so Tom Hudgin, a very good pilot and longtime friend, came to help. He flew it out of Mayo Lake and brought it to Stewart flying with floats instead of wheels. The wonder of wings thrilled me every time I went flying. I had been told that bush flying was hours and hours of boredom punctuated by moments of sheer terror, but I didn't find that to be totally true for me. I have logged 916 hours, and some not logged, during a 16-year period and have never had an hour of boredom, but there have been a few moments that were close to terror.

CHAPTER 11

Flying C-GSMW (Gulf Sierra Mike Whiskey)

(1986-1989)

I t was wonderful having wings. I spent a lot of time flying SMW while I built hours and prepared for my pilot license test. I was using a Piper Tomahawk, GANL (Gulf Alpha November Lima) in Whitehorse to do my official training and would use it for my test flight. It was practice, practice, practice, over and over, until my instructor was confident that I would pass the flight test. On the scheduled day, the DOT (Department of Transportation) examiner went with me to the plane and we did the "walk around," inspecting the usual things before a flight. We got in the plane and took off.

Everything went well until he pulled power and declared, "Engine failure." I went through the normal routine of engine restart, radio calls and passenger briefing while I looked for a suitable landing sight. The Alaska Highway was below us, off to one side, so I knew it would be easy to put down. The instructor asked me where I intended to land so I just said, "on the Alaska Highway." That wasn't good enough since he wanted to know exactly where on the Alaska Highway because it is over one thousand miles long. I pointed to a small bridge and told him that I would land just beyond the bridge.

Everything went as planned. I was getting lower and lower, and I started a slide slip to lose altitude faster as I approached my landing spot. By now as cars were starting to pull over to the side of the road, the examiner said, "Go around." His instruction made no sense to me because I knew I wasn't allowed to add throttle, and I was way too low to be able to make a 360 degree turn and get back to the road to land. As I kept getting lower and more cars pulled off to the side, he said again, "Go around," with a loud voice. So while trying to focus on keeping the airplane lined up with the road and getting very low, I said, "I can't, I'm too low." He shouted, "Pull up! Pull up!" So I added power and began climbing.

While we climbed up to altitude, he explained that when he said "go around" he meant to pull up and go around. My instructor had never used the "go around" instructions, so I took it literally and didn't follow my examiners instructions. I passed the test in spite of the misunderstanding and learned some lessons as well. Number one: always give clear instructions and never assume the other person knows what you mean. Number two: if instructions don't make sense, ask for clarification.

With my license in hand I could now fly with other people on board. I will never forget my first passenger, Mary Persinger. She needed to come out of Trapline 106 on the McMillan River. It was a nice flight, about an hour long over the mountains east of Stewart Crossing. Since SMW was on floats I could land on the river. I don't know if she was nervous or not, but she got in the airplane and didn't show any sign of fear as we took off to fly to Stewart Crossing and landed on the river.

Taylorcraft BCI2D on floats on the Stewart River, Yukon Territory

I made many flights to the McMillan River over the next 6 years. I bought skis for SMW so I could fly in the winter and land on the snow. One winter day I had gone in with some freight. When I took off to head back home after unloading everything, I circled up to get altitude to cross the mountains. Everything was fine, but when I leveled off at about 9000 feet, the engine started sputtering and backfiring. I immediately pulled the throttle back and headed down towards the snow-covered strip that I had just left. I landed fine and then checked the fuel, spark plugs, and air filter. Everything looked good so I tried again. Climbing was fine but when I leveled off at 9000 feet, it started running terribly.

I was not going to make the one-hour flight home over the mountains with the engine running like this. So I turned back again and landed on the snow strip on the McMillan. The Persingers and Carpenters came out again. This time I went to the SBX-11 radio and called Betsy at Stewart Crossing. She got on the phone and called the mechanic that always maintained SMW. I explained everything and he gave me some good pointers to check on. After going back to the airplane and checking everything over again and finding nothing, I decided to pull the fuel line going to the carburetor. It was a rubber line and came from the fuel shut off and sediment bowl. I had cleaned the sediment bowl earlier and it was clean. The line went horizontal except for a short space where it dipped down and back up again. I disconnected the line at the carburetor, and a small amount of fuel came out because the fuel was shut off. I asked one of the men to go inside and push in the fuel shut off knob. I held a small bowl to catch anything that might come out of the line. I was shocked when a small blob of yellow-looking jelly came out with the fuel. It took a bit to figure out what it was. Then I remembered I had used Seal-All to fix a very small crack in the fuel tank. As I worked it into the tank, it had mixed with the fuel and slowly accumulated in the tank. While I climbed, it stayed back from the carburetor, but when I leveled off it would flow into the filter at the inlet and plug it. I cleaned everything out again and left for home. The problem was fixed.

The wind could be really strong in the Whitehorse area, so it was a good place to learn to fly. I got lots of practice landing and taking off in windy and gusty conditions. Since there were mountains all around, it could be very rough flying at altitude as well. One summer day our son, Steven, and I were going to fly SMW from Whitehorse to Stewart Crossing. While I was getting a weather briefing, someone casually remarked about wind shear north of town on the east side of Pilot Mountain. This was exactly where we would be flying, but it didn't sound too bad, so we prepared for the flight home. The weather was actually very good with high clouds. We were about 3500 feet ASL (Above Sea Level) approaching the east side of Pilot Mountain as we flew north towards home. It was a bit bumpy and I had forgotten about the wind shear. Suddenly, I was reminded of what I heard in the weather office. SMW was being pushed up so hard and fast that I could hardly lift my hand to bring the throttle back. With the engine at idle and the nose pointed down, the airspeed picked up quickly, but we just kept climbing. Then it changed. A big bang and the updraft became a down draft. I thought the wings were going to come off. Now I added full power and brought the nose up to try to climb and keep from being pushed down. This happened three times; each time I thought the wings were going to be ripped off. I wanted to land but was not going to go back through those conditions, so we continued on to Stewart Crossing. I checked the plane over very carefully after landing but found no damage. Steve and I were both scared, but didn't want to show it, so the other wouldn't get afraid.

I had a few issues with SMW, so I took it to Whitehorse and landed at a strip just north of town at some friends' house. They had a hanger where I could easily work on it myself. The airplane was very simple with no charging system or starter and no electronics. When I wanted to start it I simply primed it, pulled the prop over a few times, turned the switch to the left magneto, and pulled the prop again to get it started. The brakes were always set, and throttle set low. Then I would crawl in, turn the magneto switch to both, release the brakes, and taxi away.

On this particular day it was hot, and I was going to land on the road in front of the house at Stewart Crossing. It was fairly easy because the bridge was out of the way: just drop in over the guard rails, stay in the center of the road, and miss the traffic signs. There were several lanes I could turn into and I could see traffic a long way off before I landed, so it was never a problem. As I took off from the dirt strip, I noticed some goffer holes and tried to avoid them as it bounced the plane a bit. The takeoff went well, and the flight was good. The approach to land was perfect: sailed over the guard rails, kept everything in the center of the road, and just as I slowed down and the tail wheel touched the pavement, everything started to shake. I pushed in the yoke to take weight off the tail wheel but eventually the tail had to come back down. As soon as it touched again, the shaking started. Then I lost steering. The only way I could steer it now was with the individual brakes which were terrible on a Taylorcraft because they were mechanically operated with cables. I soon lost all control, zig zagging from side to side down the highway, still going pretty fast, and heading for the ditch towards some big tall trees. I remember calling out for help. "Jesus!" was all I had time to say. It all happened so fast.

Suddenly, I was stopped right up at the trees and the engine was still running. I quickly shut it down and crawled out. The propeller was inches from the trees, and one wing had hit a telephone pole putting about a 4-inch dent in the leading edge. It was amazing; no other damage! Don Lefler and my brother Mark came running from the gas station that we had and helped push it back to the shop. I parked in front of the house and repaired it before the next flight. The problem with the tail wheel was that one of the springs connecting it to the rudder had broken during takeoff, so I had no tail wheel control. I reminded myself again, "Whosoever shall call on the name of the Lord, shall be saved." This is true in more ways than we know.

One winter Don Lefler and I were going to fly out to the Plata airstrip for a visit with Tom and Carolyn Plunket who were trapping there. The forecast was good for the day but showed snow coming in late that evening. After fueling up we headed out over the mountains to the northeast, confident that we would be back before the snow came. The flight went well, and we landed on the frozen dirt strip. I didn't have skis at that time, so we flew on wheels. After landing we walked about 200 yards to the cabin which was located in heavy timber. We had lunch, talked, and was having a very good time when we looked outside and noticed that it was starting to snow. We quickly packed up, got to the airplane started up, and took off heading to Mayo. It was easy to follow the creek as we stayed low. The snow started to get very heavy and all I could do was see directly down. So I quickly turned around and headed back up the creek to find the Plata airstrip. Thankfully, we found it and landed safely. We stayed the night while it snowed and snowed.

We woke the next morning to 12 inches of snow and minus 40 degrees. I knew this would be a challenge. I always carried a heater with me as well as engine and wing covers which we had put on when we arrived back during the snow. So I opened things up and lit the heater to warm the engine. It took several hours before I was ready to start it. The sky was blue and still minus 40 when I got the engine started. Don and I loaded our stuff and tried to take off. The strip is very hilly, going downhill to the west, which was good. I taxied to the east end and started to take off. The deep snow just held me back and I could not come close to reaching flying speed. I turned around and with full power attempted again, and again, each time packing down a bit wider track and picking up more speed. After the fourth or fifth attempt, I managed to get airborne. It felt so good to climb up into a cloudless sky. It would be about an hour and twenty-minute flight to Mayo. As usual, I was monitoring ground speed by keeping track of our location on the map and checking all the gauges. Slowly it dawned on me that the oil pressure was dropping, and the oil temperature was rising. I made a quick note of our location and time remaining in the flight. I continued monitoring and soon concluded that we would run out of oil pressure before we reached Mayo. I was concerned with the amount of oil that the engine had because the oil temperature was rising. It was minus 40 and I did not want to have the engine quit when we were forty miles from Mayo.

I had an idea. I knew there were some cabins at No Gold Creek where the Randolph and Lucas families lived. They were gone now but at least we could make it there and put down on the snow-covered river. We would at least have a cabin to go to and wait for someone to come for us. So I explained to Don that our oil pressure would just get us there, and we would have to set down in the snow. Since we were on wheels, it was very likely that we would nose over in the deep snow. But that would not be a difficult situation since we would be going very slowly, and the deep snow would cushion us. We arrived at No Gold Creek with about two pounds of oil pressure, so I told Don that we had to stop. He said he would pray, but wanted me to keep my eyes open, my hand was on the throttle ready to cut the power. He just said something very simple like, "God we need oil pressure." I was ready to cut the power and glide down to the river but glanced down one more time at the gauge. I was shocked as I watched it start climbing from about two pounds of oil pressure to seven pounds. I told him to look at the gauge and said that we could make it to Mayo. I left the power on and turned to follow the river towards Mayo. The gauge started dropping again and when we landed at Mayo, it was just above zero. It looked like somehow, God had put more oil in the engine while we were flying. When I shut off the engine and checked things over, the front seal had gotten pushed out because of the cold, and oil had been leaking out from the time we left Plata. There was about one liter of oil out of five left in the crankcase.

One summer my brother Galen brought his family up to visit us. I wanted to take him out to the outposts so he could see some of the places I was flying. The airplane was parked in the slough behind our house, so it was easy to access. We loaded up and took off from the river. It was a hot day so climbing out was a bit slow, but the flight was good. We had a good day and by the time we headed home the wind had picked up a bit. So flying around the mountains was going to be a bit rough. Sure enough, as we were coming past Mayo, Galen didn't look so good so I asked him if he was ok, knowing that if it was rough here, it was really going to be rough as we got closer to Stewart Crossing. We could land in Mayo and have someone come up with a car and get him. He said he was fine, but he looked worse.

I told him that there were some sick sacks in the glove box in front of him and on the right. I forgot to tell him that the glove box door was spring loaded. I remembered the spring when I saw him clawing the door with his right hand and saw the door go shut before he could get his hand in to get a sick sack. There was a yoke for flying from the right seat in front of him, and it was also in his way. I let go of my controls, reached over, held the door open, and grabbed a sick sack. Poor Galen was really sick now as the plane was veering off to the left by itself, while I got the sack for him. I got the plane under control again while he put the sick sack up tight to his mouth. It was too tight to his mouth so when he proceeded to violently empty his stomach contents into the sack, there was no place for all the air to go. He blew out the bottom of the sack. Now the contents of the sack were blown across my lap and hit my side of the cabin. We both were sitting in it as well. My poor airplane would never be the same. We landed on the Stewart River and taxied up to the shore. His wife and daughters were there waiting. Galen handed them the dripping sack so it could be dealt with. They felt so sorry for him, and so did I. I know what it's like to be sick too. I still love my brother!

The little Taylorcraft served us well even though it had no lights or radios. Navigation was simple with a compass and directional gyro driven by vacuum. I carried a small battery-operated radio with me when I had to fly to Whitehorse, so I could be in communication with the control tower. Almost all the flying was "bush" flying so the radio rarely got used. I loved flying on floats. Since SMW was fairly underpowered for floats, I usually had to take off by lifting one float out of the water at a time. Otherwise, it wouldn't lift off the water. This skill that Tom Hudgin taught me served me well many times when I had a larger airplane, and it helped to get out of tight spots when heavily loaded.

I loved the freedom of flying to bush strips with no radio operators telling me when and how to land. It was just "have a look, line up, and set it down." One time this attitude got me in trouble in Whitehorse. It was winter and I was on skis. The ski strip was located on the far south end off to the right side. I didn't like it because I always had to taxi all the way back to the north end where I would park. I had called flight services, then gotten switched to the control tower, and they had cleared me to land on the ski strip. But while I was coming in from the north, I noticed that someone had taken off beside the runway on the north end. I concluded that if they can do it, so can I. So I pulled the power back, set up a steep side slip and landed right where the other plane had left its tracks. Beautiful, I thought. Now I can just taxi right over to the hanger. Then the control tower come on the radio and demanded to know why I had not followed his instructions. I tried to explain, but he wasn't impressed with my logic. After that conversation I knew I had better never, ever, do that again.

The beautiful thing about bush flying is that you never know the excitement that may be just ahead. I was going in to No Gold Creek late one evening while on floats. It was getting dusk so I wanted to land as close as I could, which meant coming in over a very small island and landing towards their cabins. The brush was about six feet tall on the island, and

I had cut the engine to an idle as I dropped down and came over the brush at the edge of the water. I was very quiet as I approached, so the dozen or so mallard ducks that were sitting just in the water's edge didn't hear or see me until I was very close. I surprised them and they flew up vertically right in front of me, relieving themselves as they went. Thankfully, I never hit any of them. The front of SMW looked like a barnyard until I cleaned it off the next morning.

Another time I was flying into Russel Post in the winter. Bill Ritchie was with me and we had a beautiful flight. After circling over the snow strip that was located between a large island and the mainland, it all looked good. I made my approach over the trees just down river and made a good landing at the very beginning of the strip. We were slowing down nicely as the skis skimmed over the packed snow. Then I was startled to see a big moose step out of the island and onto the airstrip and start running just ahead of me. I started encouraging the moose, "Go moose, go, go, go," as I was catching up to him. He didn't want to leave the strip because it was easier running there than in the deep snow on the sides. The nose of the airplane was up so Bill couldn't see him, so he kept asking, "What's wrong, what's wrong?" All I could think was, if the prop hit that moose, there would be moose hair and hooves everywhere. I got within about 10 feet of him before the plane slowed itself down and the moose ran ahead.

CHAPTER 12

Kilo Yankee Kilo

(1989-1992)

C essna makes a good airplane. The Taylorcraft was good, but small and slow. It was hard to get out of tight places on floats, because it only had a 90-horsepower engine. When there was no wind, it could be difficult to get off the water. I learned to be very careful on skis as well, especially when the snow got a bit sticky in the spring. In the winter it was difficult at times because when on skis, I could only land on snow. There was no option for a wheel/ski combination.

I began to look for a larger airplane with more power and the option of having hydraulic wheel skis, as well as having four seats instead of just two. I knew I would not be able to buy something else until I sold SMW because of the extra cost. A good friend, who saw the need to upgrade, told me that he would finance the next plane; so I should find one and then sell the smaller one after buying the new one. Then I could take the money from the sale of SMW and put it toward the loan. I started looking and found one in Saskatchewan. With the financing all in place, the owners of KYK flew it to Whitehorse to meet me and give me a chance to check it out.

It was a good model, a 1959 Cessna 180B. I liked it from the start. At the time it was on hydraulic wheel/skis. It did not have floats, so I would need to get them later. The first thing I did was put on a Sportsman STOL (Short Take Off and Landing) kit. It really stabilized the airplane at low speeds which was very helpful with short field work. My first flight after the STOL kit was put on was a bit tricky. I took off in Whitehorse to fly a circuit or two, but just after takeoff the airspeed indicator quit working. I had enough experience with this airplane that I could just about tell the correct landing speed by the sound of the airplane. So after landing I took it back to the shop to check it out. Somehow some dirt or dust had gotten into the pitot tube and blocked the line. It was easy to clean and fix. I had many enjoyable flights with KYK and some that were not.

Cessna 180B KYK fueling up at the airport in Mayo, Yukon

KYK with a new paint. Fueling up with jerry
cans while on the river at Mayo, Yukon

While flying on wheels one summer, I flew into Kalzas
Mountain air strip. It wasn't far from home, but it was 4000
feet ASL (Above Sea Level). I was bringing out Pat and Randy
Randolph, who had been doing some prospecting, and taking
them back to No Gold. I had flown them often and always
enjoyed being around them. But this day it was hot, and they
had lots of stuff to bring out. I was concerned. I had flown on
hot days and from high altitude strips, but never high and hot
at the same time. As I watched the load coming on, I finally
said, "Enough, we can't take any more." Sometimes it could
be difficult to stop loading, because people always had more
stuff than I could take. I needed to plan my takeoff. There was
a very little bit of wind from the south, but the airstrip went
uphill that way. Also, the mountain was there so I would have
to start turning almost immediately after take-off. I chose
to take off downhill with a very slight tail wind and with the
valley dropping off at the end of the airstrip. I would not need

to climb or turn. I only needed to get off the airstrip and climb about four feet to get over a dirt berm at the end. I walked back from the end of the airstrip marking off the distance I would need to have in order to stop if I wasn't airborne. I drug out a log from the trees and laid it in plain view so I could easily see it. If I wasn't flying by that point, I would abort the take-off. After taxiing to the opposite end of the airstrip and pushing the airplane backwards into the brush as far as I could, we got in, satisfied that it was all laid out. I did not put on flaps because of the extra drag it would cause while we picked up speed. I would wait until I was at flying speed, then add flaps, and raise the nose. Off we went—full power, tail in the air as soon as possible, and picking up speed nicely it seemed. I was busy with my hand on the throttle and my eyes watching the airstrip, my airspeed, and looking for my log. Suddenly, I went past the log and I wasn't flying yet. I was committed, ready or not. So I kept the tail up and full throttle but my hand was now on the flap handle. Just at the very end, I pulled back on the yoke and at the same time I pulled flaps. The stall warning horn was blaring loud as the airplane hung, barely flying, at the stall speed. We just cleared the berm and I quickly pushed the yoke in, lowered the nose of the airplane, and picked up airspeed as we headed down into the valley. My hands were wet with sweat. Randy asked what that horn was about. I told him it was just an indicator letting us know that we were at flying speed.

When flying in the North, you could encounter the most unusual circumstances. I was hauling some freight to No Gold Creek one winter. The front seat on the right side was out, as well as the yoke, so I had more space for the load. It was full, but at the last minute, Betty Lucas wanted to put in her small dog as well. She said he was real nice and had flown before, so I just put him on top of the load. As I was nicely flying along, the dog crawled up from the back over top of the freight and laid down on top of the interment panel - right in front of me. I couldn't see out the front, so I very gently nudged him off the instrument panel and back on top of the freight. Soon he took his place in front of me again. So again, I gently nudged him back to the freight. The third time he came forward to claim his spot in front of me, I was lined up for landing on a very short narrow snow strip. There was no time for gentleness. I simply grabbed him and threw him to the back of the plane. After landing and taxing to unload, I looked around to find the dog huddled way in the back in a corner. He was looking at me with huge eyes like only small dogs can do. I don't think he ever figured out why I treated him so rough. If only he knew; he could have gotten us both killed.

Another time flying dogs was totally different. When I carried big dogs, I would chain them down in the back with their heads fairly close to the floor. I had Don Lefler with me since we were going to the trapline for his son Jason. We had some freight with two dogs. I tied down one on my side and Don tied down the other on his side. I was always very careful, as I had seen dogs' chains come loose and then they were free to move around. I didn't like that. The other problem with big dogs in a small airplane is that they start breathing heavily, their tongues hang out, they slobber a lot and their breath stinks awful. On this trip the dog behind Don got his chain loose and got his head up to where he could just put it over Don's shoulders. There was no where to go, so the dog slobbered over both of Don's shoulders and soaked him. It looked horrible and smelled worse. Poor Don!

Cats were different! If I had to have a cat in the airplane with me, I always put it in a box and taped it shut. Of course, there were enough holes in the box so the cat could breath but not escape. I learned this lesson from someone else's mistake. I will not give his name so no one will think bad about him. He was flying over the Yukon mountains with a cat—a very nice, calm, friendly cat. After flying several thousand feet above the ground for a while, the nature of the cat changed somehow. It started running counterclockwise around the cabin in circles—from the back, to the front passenger side, onto the instrument panel in front of my friend, along the pilot door, and into the back again—over and over again. My friend got concerned because he had a fairly long flight ahead of him and couldn't catch the cat or make it stop. All he could think to do was to pop open his side window, so when the cat came around the next time, it would get sucked outside. He opened the window and the cat was suddenly outside several thousand feet above the ground. Immediately, he felt bad about opening the window but was comforted as he thought, "Oh well, at least he will land on his feet." So I learned two simple rules for flying with cats: one, simply put it in a box, and two, tape it shut.

There were times I would land KYK on the road at Stewart Crossing and park behind the shop. It was handy to do minor repairs and clean things up since it was right by the house. I didn't think much about it since I had seen other places in Yukon and Alaska were planes were parked beside houses that were far from an airport. I knew it wasn't illegal to land or take off from a road. One summer when I had the plane parked behind the shop, the RCMP stopped by while I was working in the shop. I wasn't unusual to see them because they often stopped by to get gas for their vehicles. After we talked a bit, he asked me how often I used the road as a runway. I explained that it wasn't often since I only wanted to do something to the airplane, and that I was always careful. After he explained that it really wasn't "illegal" for me to use the road as a runway, he asked if I knew what I would be charged with if I caused an accident. I had never thought about it. He told me that if there was an accident with me in the airplane on the road, I would automatically be considered the one at fault and would be charged with driving an over width vehicle without a permit. While landing was never hard because I could see traffic in all directions as I came over the bridge, taking off was a bit different. He concluded the conversation by offering to block traffic any time I wanted to take off. The next time I flew off the road, I took them up on the offer. It actually did feel safer with them sitting on the road with their lights flashing.

KYK sitting behind the shop at Stewart Crossing, Yukon

The Cessna cost a lot more to fly than the Taylorcraft, so one summer I decided to get my commercial license and fly with a company in Whitehorse. After I had the commercial license, I checked out the details of working with a charter company, with my plane based in Stewart Crossing. I started to have some complications when I would be scheduled to fly, and due to weather, I couldn't. The flight would get moved to the next day when I often had work booked in the shop for auto repairs. I began to make a common mistake of flying in marginal weather conditions due to a tight schedule. This happened for the last time one spring day.

The floats had only been on for a short time and four men with a bunch of gear wanted to go from Mayo to Bonnet Plume Lake. It would be an easy flight but would take two trips. We hadn't been on the lake yet, but I thought it should be open enough to land on the water. The winds were very strong from the west that morning as I left Stewart Crossing to go to Mayo to pick up passengers and gear. I took off into the wind, going down river, and was off the water really quick. The trip east to Mayo was fast, due to the strong tail winds. I set up to land going down river and facing the dock at Mayo, expecting a fairly strong cross wind. Normally, this wouldn't have been a problem, except the wind was coming over a very high bank with tall trees on it and causing a big down draft right before I touched down on the water. So instead of touching down on the water with the airplane nose up and landing on the back of the floats, I landed flat and hard, resulting in excessive drag on the water and the airplane tending to tip over on its nose. I had just pulled the throttle off, but my hand was still there, so immediately I added full power and pulled the yoke as far back as I could. The airplane jerked forward and for a moment I thought we would nose over, but with full power and the yoke back, it just held while it skipped forward a couple times. Finally, the nose stayed up and with the airspeed down, I was able to stabilize and taxi to the dock.

After loading two men and some gear, we headed east to the lake. When we flew over the west end of the lake, it was obvious that the wind had opened up a fairly good space for landing. The ice was nicely out of the way. I landed and taxied to shore, unloaded, and headed back through the mountains to Mayo for the second load. While flying back a small, light rain shower turned into a bad down pour with very gusty winds. I had very poor visibility and worked hard to maintain control. The storm settled out and I got back to Mayo. The weather was better on the return, but when I got to the lake, the wind had shifted and was bringing all the ice back into the area I had landed on earlier. After circling and looking it over, I thought I had enough room to get in. The landing went fine but I was in a hurry to get out before the open area was clogged with ice.

I quickly pushed off without doing a "run up," just added power, and headed out. Just before I got "on the step," I hit a very large piece of ice that had floated into the small area I had landed in. I cut power because there was not enough room now for take off. I quickly taxied to the southwest corner of the lake and tried to take off in another small open area. Thankfully, I was able to get off and fly out over a swamp to gain some airspeed before starting the climb to altitude. It had been a tough, stressful day, but as I flew back to Stewart Crossing, the weather had cleared up nicely and the winds had stopped.

As I flew home at about 6000 feet ASL, I relaxed and enjoyed the beauty. I reviewed the events of the day, and it was quiet, except for the hum of the engine. A question from God demanded an answer from my heart, "Why are you doing this?" I had to answer that I had made it about me. I loved flying and seeing the beauty of the North. The extra money I could make was always useful to make upgrades to the airplane. Suddenly I didn't feel very safe. Very shortly after that I stopped flying commercially, only using the airplane for the Lord's work.

It is always good to know that when you serve God and look after His work, He looks after you, protects you, and gives you the things you need. I didn't approach flying as a service to God or some sort of spiritual activity, but simply used what I had to help others—whether it was the airplane in the Yukon or the boat on the Finlay River.

One afternoon I was going to fly Amelia Huntly into No Gold to visit the Randolphs. The airplane was on floats, so it was tied up behind the house on the Stewart River. The flight was only about thirty minutes long, but I wanted it to go perfectly because she had been in a very serious small airplane accident several years previously where some people were killed. I checked everything over very carefully preparing for this flight. The takeoff went perfect and as we leveled off at about 4000 feet ASL, the engine suddenly shuddered and a puff of smoke came from in front of the airplane blowing over the windscreen. It happened so fast that I wasn't sure of what I had seen. I just hoped that Amelia didn't notice. I remained very alert. Suddenly, it happened again. We were about halfway there but I wanted to get as close to home as possible, especially if we were going to have engine trouble. As calmly as I could, I said to her, "I think we will turn around." As I turned, I throttled back to go easier on the engine. We followed the river going home just in case the engine quit. If so, we could land on the water. We made it back, l landed safely, and tied up at the dock. I called my friend Ed Kozystko, who was an airplane mechanic and came to Stewart Crossing during the summer. We removed the cowling and started pulling the engine apart. After he had the cylinders off, he came and told me that the valves in one cylinder would have lasted about two more minutes before they broke. Another cylinder had a piston that he said wouldn't have lasted five minutes! I was thankful it held together long enough to get us home. Ed did lots of work on my airplanes and would never let me pay him for any of his time. The last time I tried to pay him, he said, "I watch what you do with your airplane, and this is the small part that I can do to be a help."

Ed Kozystko and me just chatting

At times I would land on the road in front of the shop at Stewart Crossing and park the airplane by the house. It gave me a chance to clean, polish or do other things to it without having to drive to the airport. It always gave me a nice feeling when I would walk out of the house and see the airplane sitting there. After just admiring the airplane one very windy, spring day, I got a call from the RCMP at Pelly Crossing telling me that my friend Tom Hudgin had asked them to call me and let me know that he had been in an airplane accident. He was at the nursing station they told me, and he would be alright but was being medevacked to the Whitehorse hospital. They informed me that he had been in an accident with his single engine Otter while flying out of the Pelly Crossing airstrip.

I could hardly believe that Tom would have an accident; he had thousands and thousands of hours of flying time and had never damaged anything. He had instructed me on many check rides as well as trained me for my float endorsement. He always said, "If you follow the rules you will never get hurt." I looked up to Tom and believed what he said. They told me he wasn't hurt too bad and would be ok. After he got to Whitehorse, I called his wife to see how he was. She said he was burned quite badly.

A day or so later I drove to Whitehorse to see him. He looked awful. We talked about a lot of serious things for the couple days I was there. I drove back home and as I parked in front of the house, I looked at the airplane but saw no beauty. I was only upset because an airplane had almost killed my good friend. About two weeks later I was going to take my friend, Gary Rehemier, out to Russel Post on the McMillan River. The water was low and since I didn't have floats I would land on the gravel bar. I had done it before, and while it was on a bit of a curve and sloped towards the river, it wasn't bad. We took off from the road and headed out for the one-hour flight. We got over the mountains and descended into the valley, heading for the gravel bar. I circled over the bar to make sure that no logs had floated up during high water and then came around to do a slow approach and fly by. It looked good so I circled around and lined up for landing. I didn't pull off the power but did another fly by. Circling around again and lining up for landing again, I could not pull off the power and commit to landing. As I went around again, I realized that all I was thinking about was Tom's crash, and I had to put it behind me and land the airplane. I came around and lined up again, this time forcing myself to pull off the power and land the airplane. I don't remember how smooth the landing was, but for me, it was extremely difficult to just go through the process once again. Tom recovered and is still flying over 25 years later.

CHAPTER 13

Echo Gulf Bravo

(2005-2008)

As changes in life came, so did the flying. KYK was sold and for a few years I didn't have an airplane. When I wanted to fly, I would rent an airplane from a local flying school. Normally it was a Cessna 172, very slow and expensive to rent. Since it appeared that it would have some use, I looked for another airplane to buy that would be cheaper to fly and would not need floats or skis. I found a nice Piper PA28-140 with lots of performance modifications on it. Since we were living in Whitehorse now, I had to park it at the airport and deal with controlled airspace and a lot tighter controls.

All the modifications on EGB made it a very nice, small, four-place airplane, with enough fuel for almost 5 ¾ hours of flying. Most of the long trips were between Fort St. John and Whitehorse. Normally, it was about 4 to 4.5 hours of flying depending on winds aloft, and if weather permitted us to go direct over the mountains.

One spring afternoon in May 2007, Betsy and I planned on flying to Fort St. John from Whitehorse but got delayed due to a frontal system moving from west to east along our intended route. I watched the weather and was tracking the system. It looked like we could just go a bit south of our normal route and we would be behind the system. Reports looked pretty good as we left Whitehorse heading in the general direction of Dease Lake, B.C. Everything was going well, except that about the time we got in the Dease Lake area, we discovered that the system had almost stopped moving. It appeared we could just go a bit farther south and get around it. It sort of worked, but then we were surrounded by snow showers and had to work our way around those. We had good visibility but were not making a lot of headway in the direction we wanted to go. As we made our way through the mountains and around the snow showers, we finally made our way into the Finlay River Valley just south of Fort Ware. It was nice familiar country, but we could not get over the mountains to go direct to Fort St. John. So we headed down Williston Lake to the Peace Arm. It felt good to see Hudson's Hope and have a road under us, as fuel was starting to get low in both tanks. I pulled the throttle back to save fuel and made our way, followed the road due to low clouds, and safely landed in Fort St. John after flying 5.4 hours. It felt really good to get out of the airplane and touch the ground. The next morning there were several inches of snow on the ground.

Flying above the mountains in Alaska with EGB

Another flight from Whitehorse to Fort St John was quite different. The sky was clear all along our route over the Rocky Mountains. On this trip two of our grandchildren, Blake and Whitney, were with us. We left Whitehorse and started our climb going directly to Fort St. John. It was cool so we could climb easily, and it wasn't long before we were up to twelve thousand feet, heading for the mountains. We started our descent as we approached the foothills on the east side of the mountains. That is when we became aware that Whitney had a bit of a cold and was a bit congested. Her ears started to hurt as we descended towards Fort St. John. I had already contacted flight services and informed them of our route and time of arrival. It was very apparent the pain was getting worse as we descended, so I leveled off, hoping that the pain in her ears would let up. I finally had to inform flight services that we were going to have to fly over and make our decent very gradual as we had a passenger with lots of pain in her ears. I think we flew about thirty miles out past Fort St. John before the pained lessened. We turned around and descended to land at Fort St. John.

The most fun flight with this airplane was taking Dad up to Braeburn Lodge located on the east end of Braeburn Lake which is on the North side of Braeburn Mountain. This was an old stopping-off place for early travelers going up the Dawson Trail. They had a few rooms to rent for the night and a café. They became famous for their cinnamon buns which were the size of a dinner plate, and very good. I know, because I ate lots of them. There was an airstrip, called Cinnamon Bun Strip, just across the road from the lodge so we flew up there with Dad and Mom to enjoy the view and, of course, a cinnamon bun. Dad had gotten some flying training years earlier, and it felt so good to be with him in an airplane. Dad enjoyed the flight and was shocked at the size of the cinnamon bun, which he also enjoyed. I concluded that Dad and I both love flying and eating deserts!

At Braeburn, Yukon on the Cinnamon Bun Airstrip with Dad and Mom

Coffee with Dad was always enjoyable

Another memorable trip with EGB was July 1, 2006, when Betsy and I flew back to Fort Ware. We hadn't been back for over 25 years. We called and let Jerry and Faye Seymour know we were coming. The airstrip still looked a lot like it did when we left, except it was longer and was graded much better. As we landed and taxied to the side, we were excited to see several people there waiting for us. It was a very emotional time as we reconnected with very close friends that we hadn't seen in over 25 years.

Landing at Fort Ware, B.C. Village is at the far end of the airstrip.

CHAPTER 14

Fires

Fires are always exciting. They start in different ways— sometimes expected, sometimes unexpected—but they always burn and change the conditions of things around them. These stories are about some fires I've encountered.

It was time to chore again. The cows always needed to be milked shortly after we came home from school. I was in grade 7 or 8. It was fall and I never liked to be cold while doing the chores, so I slowly pulled my sweatshirt on over my head and pulled up the hood. This one had a pocket in the front and your hands could go all the way through. It was nice because you could warm your hands together while in the pocket. Mom and Dad were on the porch as I was slowly getting ready to go out. I jammed my hands into the pocket and stopped as I felt an interesting sort of stick. I remembered I had found it in the match box when I was burning trash. It was totally white and looked like a big match, except it was covered in the same looking stuff that was on the tip of the matches. I had planned on checking it out later to see what it was. While I lingered and delayed on the porch as usual, I casually rubbed my thumbnail across the interesting stick in my pocket. The next instant I was having visions of my whole body being a mass of scar tissue as the interesting stick in my pocket ignited.

I jerked my hands from my pocket, bolted for the door, and frantically tried to run outside while pulling the sweatshirt off over my head with the interesting stick still in the pocket. I made it! The fire was out, and I wasn't scarred up or even burned. I turned around to face the noise coming from the porch. Mom and Dad were laughing and chattering about the whole thing. They hadn't seen the fire or even known anything about it. All they knew was that I took off outside, fast, like they had never seen. Dad said he knew something was wrong because I never went out to chore that fast.

Years later there was another fire. I desperately needed this one. During a winter in Northern British Columbia, I walked with my friend, Antoine Charlie. It was real cold and we wanted to make it to the cabin before dark. As the temperature kept dropping, we tried to walk faster to stay warm. The longer we walked the colder we got, and soon we began to think we may have to stop and warm up. We chatted a bit about stopping but decided we could make it since the next cabin was less than an hour away. A short while later we both knew we would have to stop and build a fire.

Our hands and feet were numb, and the cold had penetrated our clothes. We could hardly move our mouths to talk. We dropped our packs beside a dead spruce tree and started breaking off dead branches to get a fire started. That's when we realized we waited too long. We couldn't close our hands around the branches and bunch them together. We piled them together quickly as best we could. The mitts had to come off, so we could open the packsack and take out the matches. The bitter, freezing wind on our cold hand made them almost useless. I stared at my numb, stiff, hands and could barely move them. I was shocked! I hollered to Antoine for help. He was in the same condition.

I watched him closely as he dumped matches out on his pack. They were stored loosely in a pocket. With only his left-hand thumb able to bend, he put match sticks between each finger on the other hand with the match heads about two inches from the palm of his hand. He took out an axe file from his pack and slowly rubbed the matches over the file. The white tips on the ends of the matches lit instantly and he moved his hand over to the brush we had piled. The fire quickly caught, and soon we were warm. As we talked afterward in the cabin, he explained what he had done to prepare for this kind of situation: his matches were always loose and easy to get out of the pocket, and he always carried an axe file. The lesson was learned.

Unexpected fires always get your attention. While training for my pilot license, the instructor drilled for emergencies. One drill was for a fire on board the aircraft during flight. During these drills I often thought that this was probably never going to happen, but since this would likely be on the test, I should learn the drill. So we did the boring drill over and over again. If it was electrical, shut off the master switch; for engine fire, shut off the fuel. If necessary, open a vent for air, look for a place to land as soon as possible.... on and on it went.

It seemed a waste of time, until early one summer I was going to take off from Schwatka Lake near Whitehorse and fly back to Stewart Crossing. I'd loaded my stuff, filed a flight plane, fueled up, did the walk-around, and was ready to go. Since I was on floats and no one was around, I untied the plane from the dock and pushed myself out. The Cessna 180 was a good performer with the STOL kit, and it was fun to fly. With the blue sky and gentle breeze, it would be a fun trip home. As the plane moved away from the dock, I stepped onto the float and into the cabin. The engine started right up, and I started taxiing in a large circle as I contacted the control tower and told him of my intentions. I was instructed to contact the tower when off the water and enroute. Everything looked normal as I did the engine run-up and started the takeoff, holding back the yoke as I climbed on to the step and picked up speed while pushing the yoke slowly forward to keep the floats level. Slowly raising one float out of the water, then the other, we were airborne and climbing nicely.

Suddenly, the cabin filled with white smoke, burning my eyes and choking me. My response was instant. Electrical fire... master switch off! I hadn't even raised the flaps yet, so I just pulled the throttle and landed a few seconds later. I opened both cabin windows and vents. With the master switch off, the fire went out and soon the smoke cleared. It was a long slow taxi back to the dock where I tied up once again. I looked up under the instrument panel to see if I could find anything. The burned wire was very obvious; it had rubbed on a cable and caused a direct short, burning all the wires that were touching it. Thankfully, it was not a burned airplane with me inside—only burned wires.

Years later in the summer of 2010 I was helping an RV mechanic, Bob Chorney, work on an oven in a motor home. The pilot light lit fine, but the burner wouldn't light. This wasn't too unusual, as the flame sensor sometimes gets ash on it, so it won't let the safety valve open. After trying a few times, I reached back into the oven and rubbed the flame sensor with some emery cloth to get it really clean. Now I could see it well and knew it was clean. After lighting the pilot light again and turning the oven on, I waited for it to light. Still no flame on the burner.

I crouched down in front of the oven and put my face in closer so I could see if the pilot flame was high enough. I was on my knees with my back towards the front of the motor home. With bifocals it's sometimes hard to get your head at just the right distance to see clearly, so I was moving my face towards the oven and looking through the bottom part of my glasses. But I didn't know one important thing: the aluminum tube that supplied propane to the oven burner had broken off in the back of the stove. All this time the area behind the stove was filling up with propane. It reached the full point and began spilling into the oven just when I put my face in closer.

A ball of fire exploded out of the oven. I was clawing at my face trying to get the fire away while I was blown backwards and landed between the driver and passenger seat in the cab. People were hollering at me, yelling to each other, and running around the outside of the motor home. I was too dumbstruck to move. The fire had died out, so nothing was burning, but my face was really hot, and it smelled like burned hair. While I was trying to figure out what happened, I noticed my glasses were gone. I found them later about five feet outside the motor home door on the shop floor, but they were in the shape of a V. Finally, when I was able to walk, I went over to the sink and held cold, wet rags on my face. It took a long time with cold water before my face stopped burning.

For the rest of the day, I could only smell burned hair. I looked forward to getting home that evening and washing my hair to get rid of that awful smell. But even after a shower and lots of shampoo, I could still smell nothing but burned hair. Later that evening I found the problem: burned hair in my nose. So after some serious digging and plucking, the problem was fixed. I could smell normal again. It was wonderful.

CHAPTER 15

Heart Attack?

Wednesday, May 9, 2018

P ulled muscles can really be a problem. While living in Whitehorse, Yukon, I noticed that when I ran, there would often be a pain in my chest that felt like a pulled muscle. I would slow down or stop and stretch for a bit and it would go away. In the summer of 2017, a few years after moving to B.C., I tried getting back into running, but that same muscle would give me a problem every time. It would always hurt so I quit trying to run. It wasn't long until it started hurting more often and when least expected.

On Wednesday, May 9th, at our house near Baldonnell, BC, I finished using a power broom to sweep gravel out of the lawn and back on to the driveway. I could feel that muscle was really tired. After returning the rented power broom, I went to work fixing some RVs that had been scheduled for repair. I lifted a battery into place and really pulled that muscle again. I stopped for a bit, stretched, and tried to make it go away, but it just stayed. I finished getting the systems working on the motorhome and went to install a ladder on a travel trailer. After carrying the step ladder to the back of the unit, my pulled muscle kept hurting. I tried to brush it aside while I kept working.

While lifting the new ladder on the travel trailer, the pulled muscle in my chest really began to hurt. It moved down from the base of my throat, right to the middle of my chest and really hurt, covering a large area of my chest. I tried stretching and breathing deeply but nothing helped, so I quickly tried to finish the job. For the first time, I thought it might be a heart attack, but my left arm or jaw didn't hurt. I always thought your left arm hurt if you had a heart attack. Mine didn't, so I dismissed the possibility of a heart attack. After going up and down the ladder a few times, the pain got so bad I started to have to throw up, but it was just dry heaves and very painful. Now I was sure that I had indigestion as well as a pulled muscle. I could not understand this pain as I had never had anything like this in my life. I suspected something was wrong when I could no longer get up the ladder, but thankfully, the job was done, and I could go on to the next one which was a small electrical repair on a trailer tongue jack.

About an hour later the electrical job was done and I went home, exhausted. I sat in my chair and rested until Betsy got home. She noticed my lunch had not been eaten. After she asked if I had forgotten it, I just told her that I didn't feel very good and wasn't hungry. I explained my chest pain and indigestion to her. She looked at me and said she thought we should go to the hospital. I was too exhausted to argue about it so I told her I would take a shower first. While I showered, she ate supper.

After getting ready to go, I got the keys and drove to the hospital emergency. As soon as I told the lady at the desk that I was having chest pain, they took us right in and started asking questions...lots of them. They took me to a room while they kept asking Betsy questions. They hooked me up to a heart monitor, took lots of blood samples, and asked me more questions. My chest kept hurting but not nearly as badly as it had been, so I figured everything was settling down and we would be out of there shortly. But about an hour after our arrival, the doctor walked in and announced, "You have had a heart attack." My response was, "You're kidding!" My brain started calculating how long I would have to stay there before they let me go home. Since I was already feeling better but still had some pain, I thought they would keep me overnight just to make sure everything was ok. I had been given some nitro to spray under my tongue several times, and the pain was almost totally gone. But wrong again! The doctor explained that I would need to be flown out and have an angiogram to check things and fix the problem.

They transferred me to the ICU so they could monitor me better even though I was feeling pretty good. I had lots of visitors and had no problems, but when someone with a more critical problem than mine came into ICU two days later— and all the rooms were taken—I was moved back down to the emergency ward and put in a very uncomfortable bed. Everything was curtained off. There was privacy so nobody could see you, but everyone could hear you, and you could hear all of them.

I had been scheduled to fly to Kelowna on Friday afternoon, with a medevac airplane but it didn't happen. I was being watched fairly closely, and they were giving me lots of medicine. I had shots in my stomach for blood thinning and had blood samples taken every morning. Saturday morning when I woke up, something was different. I could hardly sit up or get out of bed to use the washroom; I was exhausted. I was given a better bed and also got to go outside. I was not allowed to walk, so Betsy pushed me in a wheelchair. In spite of how awful I felt, it was a wonderful feeling when family and friends would come to visit. Family was such an important part during this time. It was almost embarrassing because I had a hard time holding back tears whenever someone in the family walked into the room.

Family together, March 2010

Sunday morning after the blood work, the doctor came into the room and said that the heart enzymes were elevated again, indicating that there had been another heart attack. That explained why I was feeling so weak again. This new development got things rolling and I was told that on Monday I would be flown to Kelowna. The only problem was that since I had a second heart attack, they would have to bring along an EMT that specialized in heart problems. Betsy would not be able to go along down with me.

On Monday they got me ready for the flight. Betsy had gotten a ticket to fly down shortly after I was leaving, so she watched them load me into the airplane from the airport waiting room. Philip, who lived three hours away in Alberta, happened to be in Fort St. John, working on an airplane in a hanger near the plane that was taking me to Kelowna. When the ambulance drove up to the airplane, he came over and we got to see each other for a minute before I was loaded. Once again, family felt so good! As I was being loaded and strapped down in the airplane on the narrowest bed I have ever seen, the EMT told me over and over, "If you start to feel any pain or discomfort, tell me right away." I had been having pains but they would only last a few seconds, so I never said anything. At one point during the flight he said, "Are you having any pain?" I answered, "Yes, but it only lasts a few seconds, then goes away." He wasn't happy with me, especially after it happened a few times.

Family, July 2011

After arriving in Kelowna and getting to the hospital by ambulance, Faith, our oldest daughter, was there to meet me. Once again family felt so good and my emotions got the best of me again. The rooms there are very nice since it is a fairly new cardiac ward. They are all small but private. Betsy arrived about 10:00 that evening and stayed in the room with me. Faith stayed with a friend in town. The next day I was taken to have the angiogram. While I laid on a very hard, cold bed, they covered me with a very heavy blanket. I could see the big screen just on my left side. My right arm was shaved about half way to my elbow and I was told to not touch anything, so I just held it in the air. Moments later a man sat down on my right side and told me I would have a sensation in my wrist as they inserted the tubes in the arteries that go to my heart. That "sensation" was intense but it only lasted a couple seconds; then I felt a slight tingle as the tubes went up my arm.

By now I could see my heart on the big screen to my left. It looked like it was beating fine and I didn't see anything wrong. But the doctors did and began to insert stents. The first two went in fine and I didn't feel a thing. Then the doctor on my right side, that was doing the work, said to someone else that was there, "Get the balloon. This stent will not go in." Then he instructed someone else to give me more sedative. I was wide awake and didn't even know I had been given a sedative. Then the balloon went in and he started to inflate it in the artery that was blocked.

If the sedative was doing anything, I sure couldn't tell. My heart felt like it would explode. The doctor on my right shouted, "Hold still!" I said, "I am." He said, "No, you're not! Your foot is shaking, and I'm connected to your heart. HOLD STILL!" That's when I realized that my right foot was shaking violently back and forth. Since I didn't want him to pull my heart out through the artery in my right arm, I held perfectly still for the rest of the time. The balloon worked and they were able to get in the third and final stent. The three arteries that had been 90% blocked were now wide open. Back in my room, I was very thankful for modern medicine and the latest medical equipment. Only a few years ago it would have been open heart surgery. Recovery would be very fast with this procedure. One more night in the room and I was discharged to fly home the next day.

Wednesday was a long and very tiring day but it felt so good to be home again. On Friday, Jewel flew up and spent 12 days with us. What a wonderful time of recovery I had with family! I was sort of pampered and got to have lots of time to just sit and visit.

Going through the difficulty of a heart attack has made me adjust several things in my life. What our brains tell is may or may not be true, but the heart never lies. Since the heart never lies, it is something to be guarded. Out of it comes our perspective on all the issues of life. When I let my heart remain connected with God my heart remains true and guides me on the right paths of life. On the other hand, if I start choosing to go on an untrue path my heart will eventually adjust to my choices and become deceived making me feel quite comfortable living on the wrong path of life, far from God. "Be diligent about keeping your heart because out of it come all the issues of life" (Proverbs 4:23).

CHAPTER 16

Serious Mistakes

Most of our mistakes are made because we ignore obvious, known facts. But at times mistakes are made because we simply lack information or believe that something is true when it isn't. So when the knowledge that we have is used correctly in decision making, it can save our life. Using my imagination, if I could build a box to hold all the knowledge that I have and another box to hold all that I don't have, it is not hard to figure out which would be bigger. This presents a problem. What you know can help you succeed and live, but what you don't know can kill you. Since the box that would contain all that I don't know would be much larger, I am in real danger of getting killed.

One winter while living at Pikangikum, Ontario, Clair Schnupp flew me out to a lake and dropped me off to do some moose hunting. He said he would fly over in the morning but would just circle over to see if I was there. He wanted me to run out on the ice so he could see me, then, if he saw me, he would land. If he didn't see me, he would return later in the day. The lake was frozen, and there was about eight inches of snow, so the moose tracks were easy to follow. Before heading out on foot to follow the tracks, I dropped off my backpack and sleeping bag by a big tree along the shore, so they would be easy to find if it was dark before I got back. I set out full of energy and excited, forgetting about time. After a while, the tracks led up a fairly steep bank. The trees were burned up there so I assumed the moose would be close by.

When I reached the top I stood still and looked all around. Suddenly, I saw a bull stand up about 125 yards away. I slowly raised my 30-06 to my shoulder and shot. Just as he went down, a second one stood up. So I shot him too. After waiting a bit I went over to them. They were both dead but laying real awkward against a tree. I couldn't budge them to begin butchering them by myself. My only hope was to get help the next day. That's when I realized how late it was. It was going to be dark before I got back to my stuff at the lake, but I headed off in a hurry, working up a good sweat before I got there.

I was hungry and tired, so I cleared away some snow and made a small fire to heat up some tea and eat some food. I rolled out my sleeping bag on the small tarp it was wrapped in and started taking off my heavy clothes. My pack boots were very wet as well as the wool socks that I was wearing over my thin cotton ones. I kept my cotton socks on but stuffed the wet wool ones inside my wet boots, then crawled into the sleeping bag. It felt so good to lay down and look up at the stars. It was cold but I was warm in my sleeping bag. I fell asleep exhausted and didn't wake up until it was light, and I heard the sound of an airplane. I knew I needed to get out on the lake quickly, so I grabbed my boots and tried to pull out the wool socks that I had put in the night before. They were frozen solid and would not come out. My only option was to run out on to the lake, in the snow, in my stocking feet so Clair could see me. He landed and we got everything worked out. In all the years after that, I never put wet socks in my boots again.

One winter I was flying a load of supplies to Jason Lefler's trapline. I had fueled up since it would be about three hours of flying. After leaving Mayo and reaching cruising altitude and scanning the gauges, I noticed the left fuel tank gauge was not showing full. I kept flying but watched it carefully. Its soon became obvious that I was losing fuel from that tank and would not have enough to get to the lake and return to Mayo. I turned around and returned to check things out. After landing and taxing to the ramp, I got out to look things over. It didn't take long to find my mistake. After fueling up the tank through the filler on top of the wing, and hurriedly putting on the fuel tank cap, the small chain that kept the cap connected to the tank got twisted and stuck between the tank and seal on the cap. So when I was flying, the fuel was just getting sucked out of the tank. That mistake was never repeated.

When flying, it is always best to have decisions made ahead of time when possible. When getting information in preparation for a flight, there were rules to follow to make the "go or no go" decision. Sometimes everything looked good but there was a possibility of deteriorating weather. After considering the terrain that you were flying into as well as how many hours until dark, you would want to know ahead of time what conditions would cause you to turn around and return home. You would not want to wait until you were in a crisis to decide what to do. It is much easier making decisions when the brain is not in crisis mode. I was flying from Stewart Crossing to Kalzas Lake one summer afternoon. The clouds were low, and rain was forecast. If I couldn't fly direct, I would need to fly through a mountain pass that was fairly wide. I was flying on floats at the time. I loaded the gear and two passengers into KYK, and we left. I decided ahead of time that I would fly along the right side of the pass, so if I needed to turn around there would be lots of room. The clouds were very low as we approached the pass, but I could see through it and knew there was just enough room to fly without getting in the clouds. But I had decided ahead of time that if at any time the clouds in front of me blocked my view through the pass, I would turn around. Everything went well until halfway through the pass when the clouds formed right in front of me, and I couldn't see ahead. The decision had already been made, so we made a very sharp 180 degree turn to the left and headed back where we could see. It was a disappointing ride back home, but we made it through the next day. It's never too disappointing when good decisions keep you alive.

I had taken KYK down to Cooking Lake, Alberta, to get it painted and got in trouble on the way home for not taking information seriously enough. When flying in uncontrolled airspace in the Yukon mountains, I would fly whatever altitude was high enough for a good, smooth ride across the mountains and if possible, take advantage of updrafts on the upwind side of the mountains. I would let updrafts give me altitude so I could put the airplane nose down and gain airspeed. The problem was that your altitude never stayed the same. In some updrafts you could gain several thousand feet even with the nose down a bit. The trouble came while flying back from Cooking Lake, and I was in Edmonton controlled airspace. I was given my heading and altitude. I was to be at 4500 feet above sea level. No problem until I started to fly as if I was back in the Yukon and let the updrafts from the hot afternoon sun give me "free altitude." I trimmed the nose down and kept flying, gaining altitude, and not paying attention. But flight service was following me. I had a transponder that flight services could read as they had me on radar and knew my altitude. Suddenly, a harsh voice came on the radio and said, "KYK this is Edmonton Center; get back down to your assigned altitude of 4500 feet immediately." I had climbed and was at 5200 feet ASL. I knew better but wasn't paying attention. This could have caused serious issues because other aircraft were flying in the area at 5000 feet ASL and I was in their air space.

While driving the river boat on the Finlay River, I was asked to do some welding on the barge that brought the freight across Williston Lake. When I left Fort Ware, I put the welder in the boat to take with me, but somehow, I forgot the welding helmet. I didn't realize it until I was ready to weld. It was only a small crack and wouldn't take long to weld, so I thought I could just hold my hand over my eyes and look through a very small crack between my fingers. I thought this would keep out the worst of the welding flash and still allow me to see just a bit of my welding. The welding repair went fine, and I was sure that one really didn't have to use a helmet to weld. That night around midnight, I discovered the truth. My right eye felt like it was on fire. We were camping by the river, so I crawled out of my sleeping bag, made my way out of the tent, and got down to the river. I splashed the cold river water on my eye for a long time but got no relief. Finally, morning came, and we started our way upriver with the freight. My eye was sore for several days and things looked a bit fuzzy out of that eye after that. So I learned no matter how convinced you are that something is true, you will suffer the consequences if it is not true.

I have worked in ditches many times and never had trouble with the sides caving in. There were times that a side would cave in but never in the first 24 hours after digging. So I always felt safe laying water lines in a trench that was eight or nine feet deep. In the Yukon or Northern B.C., it gets cold in winter so we would bury lines at least eight feet deep. In the summer of 2019 while laying a water line in a trench beside a house we were renovating, I dug a trench to lay a new water line to the cistern. After finishing the trench with the backhoe, I jumped in with a shovel and leveled out the bottom so the pipe would lay flat. It looked easier to stay in the trench and pull the pipe into it than to walk up on the dirt pile and try to position the pipe from the top. That way I wouldn't be kicking dirt in the trench, and there wouldn't be a risk of tripping and falling in. In all my thinking and planning I failed to consider all the facts, some which I knew, some I didn't.

I knew it had been a very rainy summer, so the ground was very wet. I failed to consider the fact that the trench was on the side of the house where all the rain came off the roof and onto the ground. There were no rain gutters, so the ground was extremely wet. It was clay. I had no idea how extremely unstable the ground was. After being in the trench less than two minutes while reaching up to lift a pipe, the side of the trench collapsed, pinning me against the clay wall behind me.

In an instant I was buried up to my arm pits with all the air squeezed out of me. I could not suck in air except for what seemed like a teaspoon full at a time. No one was around to see what had happened. I tried to call for help, but no air. I realized that my cell phone was in my shirt pocket and after pulling the dirt away, I pulled it out to try and call Steve who lived next door. My brain wouldn't work, and I could not figure out how to use the phone. After passing out and waking up again, I tried but couldn't find the phone. It had fallen in the dirt right in front of me. This time I picked it up and managed to call Steve. He had been using his table saw and had put his phone on a bench away from where he was working. Just as I was calling, he had a thought to go check on me to see how it was going. After turning off the saw he went to get his phone off the bench. At that moment I was calling. He could hardly understand what I was saying but he knew something was really wrong, so he began running as fast as he could to find me.

His wife, Megan, and daughter, Katlyn, watched him pick up his phone and run without saying a word to them. They followed. When he found me, my face was grey and my lips blue. Thankfully, there was a shovel close by partially buried in the trench. He pulled out the shovel and began digging the wet clay in front of me to make space for me to breath. The digging was hard because of the wet, sticky clay, and he had to be very careful because he didn't know exactly how I was buried. He did not want the shovel to do more damage. Someone called the ambulance. It came, as well as a fire truck. About twenty minutes later there was a hole in front of me so I could breathe in again. I will never forget the wonderful sense of air going into my lungs.

It felt so good to breathe, that I was sure everything was fine, and all these emergency people should just go home. Nobody would listen to me, so they stayed. Even though I could breathe fine, the rest of my body was being squeezed by the wet clay and not getting blood flow. Soon my feet and legs began to hurt. Someone else was digging instead of Steve and it seemed so slow. All I wanted to do was to get my legs out of the clay, so I would push with my hands to try and get out. Nothing moved until they had dug down below my knees, then I slowly was able to get out one leg at a time.

It felt so good to be able to move and breathe again. I told the paramedics that I was fine, and they could go home now. They were smarter than me. They knew things that I didn't. One said to me, "No, we are not going anywhere. Lay on this stretcher, we are taking you to the hospital." I tried to explain to him that I felt fine, but he wouldn't listen. He said, "Listen to me. It's a miracle you are alive, but trust me, you are going to have pain like never before." So I obediently laid down on the stretcher. Moments later, my foot began to hurt. My shoes were still stuck in the trench, so I just pulled off my sock and discovered that my foot looked very bruised. The nurse at the hospital emergency ward checked me over and said, "It's a miracle you are alive." As I sat in the wheelchair the pain slowly increased. Later I got some strong pain medicine. After going home that evening and sitting the next several days in my easy chair, I discovered once again that the EMT knew more than I did. I never want to have pain like that again. The size of my box of knowledge grew just a bit, and I vowed to never go into a trench again.

CHAPTER 17

Hunting

I loved guns and hunting since I can remember. When we lived east of Cairo, Nebraska, I was in the eighth grade and had a 12-gauge shot gun that my uncle Gary Benson had given me. I would often take it to hunt pheasants or rabbits in the fall. I actually shot several pheasants in flight, and it was quite a thrill to see them fold up their wings and come crashing back to earth when they got hit. Rabbits were also fun to hunt. Both rabbits and pheasants were good to eat. Mom would always cook them for me. One Saturday while I was out looking for rabbits just behind the house in the pasture, I spotted two of them running into a brush pile. Since my shotgun was a single shot, I pulled the hammer back and got ready to shoot as I was sure they would soon come out. While I was waiting with the hammer back, the mailman came by to put our mail in the mailbox. He always left candy in our box on Saturday, so I forgot about the rabbits and headed over to the mailbox. I also forgot about the hammer that was back and ready to fire the 12-gauge shot gun. My brother Galen had also seen the mailman come, so he walked over there, too.

As we stood beside the mailbox and talked to the mailman, I rested the muzzle of the shotgun on top of my foot, sometimes lifting it to put it in on the other foot. For some reason I lifted it up and squeezed the trigger, forgetting the hammer was still back. The gun was still pointed down as it fired blasting up a large cloud of dust right between Galen and me. Neither of us got hit but we were shocked, and the mailman quickly left. Mom was in the house and heard the blast. I lost my gun privilege for a long time, but I did learn a good lesson.

One of the first times I ever went moose hunting was when I was spending time at Deer Lake, Ontario. I was going out with an older native man, so I didn't think it would be too difficult. It was winter and there was about a foot of snow on the ground. It wasn't too cold, so I wasn't concerned about having enough warm clothes. We packed a bit of food and some tea. I assumed we would return before dark because he wasn't taking a bed roll along. He did have snowshoes that he started wearing once we left the trail. I just followed along with my pack boots. I noticed right away that he had an advantage walking in the snow. I sunk in the snow with every step; he hardly sunk in at all.

It was hard work keeping up with him, so my breathing must have been pretty heavy and loud. We were just starting to follow some tracks when he stopped, turned around, and said, "Stop screaming!" Wow, I was just breathing! Breathing quietly was impossible for me when trying to keep up with an expert bush man on snowshoes while I wore heavy pack boots. As we followed the moose tracks, he kept stopping and telling me to stop screaming, over and over. I was only breathing! He was quite annoyed at me, but I couldn't help it. I had come along to help carry moose meat back to camp, and I hoped that my loud breathing wouldn't scare away all the moose for miles around.

After hours of walking and following the moose, we caught up to the moose and he shot two of them. I was really amazed to watch him and tried to help. I noticed that it was getting late, and we had a lot of work to do before we could even start the long walk back home. The first thing he did was take off his snowshoes and use them to shovel the snow off a very large area. He lit a big fire and started butchering, skinning both animals before cutting them apart. As he worked he kept moving the fire a few feet at a time. He never said a word, so I didn't ask what he was doing. I just watched and helped with whatever he was doing.

Finally, just as it was getting dark, we had a large area where the fire had been. He moved the fire one more time, then took one of the moose hides and laid it out with the hair side up over where the fire had been. We finished cutting up the meat, ate some food, and drank tea. Very little was said, and I didn't ask questions even though I had lots of them. After a while he took the second moose hide and laid it over the first one, only this one was laid with the hair side down. It had been dark for a long time, but we just sat by the fire staying warm. Finally, pointing to the moose hides, he said, "Crawl inside, we sleep here." I wasn't surprised, but the idea of sleeping between two moose hides had never crossed my mind before, and I wasn't really excited about it. He showed me how. It was easy! Just lift the hide and slide in, using the small backpack as a pillow. The smell was horrible, and the hair was very itchy, but it was warm, and I was amazed how well I slept. The next morning after having tea and bannock, we loaded our pack sacks and headed back to Deer Lake. That was the only time I was at Deer Lake and hunted with him.

I learned a lot about hunting from some great men during the years we lived at Fort Ware in Northern British Columbia. I learned the different animals' habitats, habits, and ways to successfully hunt them. We hunted moose most of the time but also caribou, goats, and black and grizzly bears. Sometimes we hunted along the rivers with a boat, and sometimes we walked up in the mountains. It was always rewarding to bring back some meat for the family as well as sharing some with old people and neighbors in the village.

During the mid-1970s, I worked with Kachika Range Outfitters guiding big-game hunters from Europe. I loved "the bush" and helping people get the game they wanted. You never knew what to expect, but I tried to always be ready for the unexpected.

We had to set up tents to sleep in as well as tents for cooking and storing supplies. I was flown in by Super Cub to Spinel Lake to set up camp so it would be ready when hunters arrived a few days later. The tents were all in a pile ready for me. I was alone, so after spending most of the day building frames for them, I stopped to rest and eat some food. I was relaxing a bit, leaning against a big tree, and almost asleep in the afternoon heat. Suddenly, I heard the most awful, loud screaming I had ever heard. I jumped up looking for my gun and trying to figure out what was happening. The screaming stopped as suddenly as it started, but my heart kept pounding. Looking around, I spotted a mother bald eagle with its young one sitting up in my tree and looking down at me. At that moment, there was not a lot of love between us. I don't think they liked me being there, and I really didn't like them screaming at me.

That year, one of my hunters wanted to get a moose. We walked about an hour to a small lake where I knew moose hung out in the fall. As we got to the west end of the lake, we spotted fresh tracks from that morning. We walked up the trail for a bit and found where he had pawed a hole and left his urine for a scent to attract cows. We checked out his tracks and concluded he had gone up on the side of the mountain. I assumed that he would return in the afternoon following his same trail and calling to attract cows. So I told the hunter that we would just wait until about 3:00 because that was about the time I expected the moose to return.

We ate our lunch and took a nap. About 2:30 I woke the hunter and told him we needed to pay attention and listen for the moose calling coming back down the trail. About ten minutes before three, we heard him grunting as he made his way towards us.

I got the hunter into position so he would be ready to shoot as soon as the moose stepped out on the shore of the lake. In just a few minutes a nice bull moose stepped out into the sunshine on the lake shore. But the hunter just looked through his scope and said, "Beautiful!" I whispered to him, "Shoot." The only response I got was, "Beautiful!" Finally, after what seemed like forever, he fired his rifle, and the moose dropped. It was 3:10. I got his attention and pointed to my watch, feeling quite proud of myself.

We cut up the moose, saving the cape and horns for the hunter. We had to save the meat as required by law. The next morning the plane came in and picked everything up and took it back to camp. I spent the morning cleaning the cape and skull. In the afternoon, my hunter wanted to do some fishing since we didn't have time to go bear hunting that day. There was a nice little creek coming into the south end of the lake, and while I had never fished there, I heard there were nice trout there. We took the boat and pulled onto shore just before the creek. I knew that trout would often feed just on the edge of a whirlpool. I told the hunter to cast right at the edge of the whirlpool. He tried but would never get his lure to the right place. I told him to watch me and then try to put his lure in the same place. My lure landed in the exact spot I told him to place his lure. Just as I said, "OK, right there," my rod bent, and I thought I snagged a log. My rod began to jerk as I tried to reel him in. It was a big one and he was fighting. After getting my fish on shore and finding it was a thirty-two-inch trout, the hunter looked at me for a long time. I guess he was trying to figure me out because things were working out like I said yesterday as well as this day. He finally said, in a heavy German accent, "You, just like God." I wanted to just say, "Thank You," but I knew all too well that within five minutes I could make a catastrophic mistake and not be like God at all.

That same summer I had another hunter who didn't think I knew anything. He would never do what I told him, and I got really frustrated. He wanted a moose, but whenever I wanted to stop and look over an open area with binoculars, he would walk off, and I couldn't find him. I would tell him to stay in a spot high in the mountains where he could see a large area and watch for moose moving through. I would be a short distance away. When I would return, he was gone, stomping through the bush, and making lots of noise. One evening he was complaining that we only sit and look and never walk to find anything. It was obvious he knew nothing about hunting moose in the mountains, but I decided that if he wanted to walk, we would walk. I would make sure that the next day when we returned home, he would not complain that we didn't walk enough. I knew the area well and planned an exhausting day for him.

We left early the next day. Instead of going around a swamp, we went right through it, so his feet were going to be wet all day. Then we headed up a valley into the mountains and over into the next valley. When we got on the back side of the mountain, we only stopped for a quick lunch. Then I told him we needed to hurry to get back to camp before dark. After we got around to the front side of the mountain and came into a big opening, I spotted a big patch of soapberries, or some people call them buffalo berries. They are extremely tart and make your mouth really pucker up. I can't stand to eat them, but I know that some people like them. So I picked a big bunch and handed them to my hunter. I told him that I don't like them, but some people do, so he might like to try them. He put the whole handful of berries in his mouth. I think he only chewed about twice before he violently spit and said, "Tart!" As we approached camp just before dark, we took a short cut through another small swamp, just to sort of finish out the day. I was fine because I was used to walking and climbing mountains, but my hunter was finally tired as he sat down in the cook tent. I felt like I finally stopped his complaining about not walking enough when, in his German accent, he said, "He nigh kilt me!"

Unfortunately, he never did get any game, although I think he could have if he would have just followed instructions.

Another year while guiding, I had a hunter from Switzerland who had crushed his ankle a year earlier and was just now walking without pain. He wanted a grizzly bear. I thought it should be fairly easy as I had been watching several of them for a few weeks. I was concerned about his ankle in the rough mountainous terrain with grizzles. His attitude was great and positive, and he seemed to know what he could do when starting up the mountain early one morning. We soon spotted a nice-sized grizzly on the edge of bunch of tall trees above us. It looked like he was eating something in a brushy area. It was hard to tell how tall the brush was since we could only see him when he stood up but not when he was down on all fours. We slowly made our way toward him, stopping when he stood up.

When we got within about 75 yards we stopped and waited. Finally, he stood up and looked around like he was looking for something. My hunter was ready and got off a good shot. The grizzly went down immediately, and I felt like it was a good shot the way the bear reacted. But a moment later, a big grizzly stood up just beside where our bear went down. It looked different. While I was trying to figure this out, another grizzly stood up not too far from us. As they went back down on four feet, others were standing up in different places. They were too close for comfort, so I decided to get myself and the hunter up on a big rock close by. It was about eight feet high, and after getting the hunter up on it, I had a hard time getting up myself.

I took the scope off the gun the hunter was using because it would be very difficult for him to shoot close range with a scope. My gun had open sights, so I was ready. We listened to the bears grunting and moving around in the thick underbrush, but we couldn't see any of them. We didn't want to shoot them anyway, unless we had to. There were at least four of them, but maybe more... we couldn't tell. I was concerned for my hunter's ankle, especially if he had to make some sudden moves.

We stood very still there for a long time before we heard and saw at least two of them moving up the mountain in the tall trees about ten yards away. After about 15 minutes of waiting and not hearing anything, it seemed like it would be ok to go and see if we could find the one we shot. After getting off the big rock, we walked around toward the area the bear went down. It seemed we were about 20 or 30 feet from where the bear should have been, when another grizzly stood up in front of us. We quickly turned around and started walking away, facing back toward the bear most of the time. He followed us about halfway down the mountain before leaving us. That night in camp we made our plan for the next day. It worked well the next morning. We carefully approached the area the grizzly was in and found him just as we thought. He had died quickly. All of the bear were out of the area, but we kept a very close lookout the whole time we skinned him and brought everything down the mountain.

Swiss hunter with his grizzly bear

One of the last hunts I did while living at Stewart Crossing, Yukon, was a late fall hunt for caribou. Betsy, Jewel, Philip, and I decided to drive the van to the base of Hungry Mountain so the walk would be shorter. Philip wanted to shoot a caribou, so we would need to get up above the tree line and spend the afternoon and early evening watching for them. By the time we got up above the trees, the wind was blowing, and it was fairly cold, but the only way we could see was to be out in the open. Betsy and Jewel tried to stay out of the wind, while Philip and I walked, and looked around using our binoculars.

Carribou on Hungry Mountain near Stewart
Crossing, Yukon, fall of 1995

Mid-afternoon we spotted several caribou coming up out of the trees and they began eating in the brush above the tree line. It looked like they were about six hundred yards away, so we slowly worked our way closer. Finally, we had to stop. I guessed they were about four hundred yards away. Since my 7mm magnum was best at shooting long distances, I would take the first shot and then Philip could go in closer to finish it off, if I brought it down. It was a nice-looking bull. As I looked through my scope I knew this was the longest shot I had ever taken and hoped for the best as I aimed high above its shoulder and squeezed the trigger. The bull went down. As Philip ran to get a closer shot, the bull tried to get up while the rest of the group of caribou ran back into the trees. Philip made the final shot and claimed the trophy. It was excellent meat and very nice antlers. After a lot of work butchering it, we loaded our pack sacks and headed back down the mountain. We were all sore and tired by the time we reached the van at dark.

Hard work cutting up the meat. Stewart
River Valley in the background.

Packing out the meat. Philip wanted the horns.

CHAPTER 18

North America and Beyond

My first experience north of the Arctic Circle came in 1982 while we were living close to Dawson City, Yukon. I drove with Eli Miller to Inuvik. The drive up the Dempster Highway to Inuvik, Northwest Territories, went through several mountain ranges before dropping down to about 15 meters above sea level when we arrived. We crossed the Arctic Circle (Lat 66.3 North) This is the point where the sun does not go below the horizon after the summer solstice, and also the point when after the winter solstice, the sun does not come above the horizon. The road is about 750 km and has very few stopping places. I found this challenging years later while driving tow truck when I worked at Klondike River Lodge.

After arriving at Inuvik, we stayed with some friends and met other Christians in the area. The next day we flew to Tuktoyaktuk to visit some others that we had met. These people amazed me with their simple approach to life. Since Tuk, (as everyone called it) sits above the 69th parallel, the sun does not set in the summer. We arrived about noon and had a wonderful time visiting and walking around the village. We ate and visited, and the sun kept shining. Around midnight we started to get ready for bed, but the sun was still shining, and kids were still outside playing. It was confusing because you couldn't tell if it was noon or midnight! The sun went in a circle overhead and the kids must have played in shifts. The sun always shone, and the kids always played. But in winter, the sun didn't shine at all for a time, and it was dark. But no matter what the environment is, these people that love the Lord all have the same focus of wanting to know Him better.

About ten years later I drove up again, this time with Russell Stendal during the winter. After arriving in Inuvik and spending the night, we left for Tuk. Since it was winter, there was an ice road all the way to Tuk. It took us down the Mackenzie River all the way to the Arctic Ocean, then out on the on the frozen ocean to Tuk. This time the sun rose just above the horizon before setting again. I was encouraged again by the hospitality and openness of the people there. Outside it was cold, but the time with these Christians was warm and wonderful. One meal I won't forget was of wild goose that had been preserved in a bucket of whale blubber, which is black. It didn't look so good coming out of the bucket, but the touch of the local cook made it absolutely wonderful.

When things started to slow down at Stewart Crossing, and we lost the lease for the shop and gas station, and many small groups in the bush were starting to close down. We moved our house about a mile south and built a shop that I would use for the repair business. I started working at a gold mine operating and repairing heavy equipment in the summer. One winter Eldred Lindon was visiting us and talked about traveling and ministering in South America. Since I had time and was looking for a change, I took the opportunity to travel with him. It was to be a two-month trip starting with a flight out of Miami. We would be in Dominican Republic, Puerto Rico, French Guiana, Argentina, Peru, Ecuador, Colombia, and Venezuela. Betsy, with Philip and Jewel, stayed with her family in Indiana.

Meeting in Argentina, January 1993

After church at Higue, Dominican Republic, January 1993

It was my first experience dealing with high temperatures and high humidity. The people we visited were amazing, loving, and always looked out for us. Our travel arrangements were very interesting: riding on the back of a small motorcycle holding on to our luggage, crowded hot buses, small taxis needing lots of repairs, large tourist buses, and large commercial airplanes. The people were always very helpful, and I always felt safe even when we were in places that were hostile to foreigners. While in Lima, Peru, I was walking in the town square with Darwin Hillario, the pastor of the local church where we were ministering. He was taking me to an ice cream shop. Cars were not allowed to drive in the main square, so people just walked everywhere. It was crowded. Darwin was walking behind me telling me which way to go, and it was difficult to make my way through the large crowded area. Eventually, I stopped and turned around and told him to lead the way and I would just follow him. He insisted that he would just stay behind me and tell me which way to go. Finally, it was so crowded that it was very difficult to push between people so we could keep moving. Again, I stopped and explained to him that it was too awkward this way; he should lead. Then he explained to me that the reason he wanted to stay right behind me was because one popular way people stole from foreigners in crowds was to walk behind them and stick a large needle into their kidneys. It made them freeze up, unable to move, so while they couldn't move, they got robbed. The thieves then pulled out the needle and moved on in the crowd never getting caught. I thanked him for walking behind me!

Some young people from the youth meetings
in Cartivia, Peru, February 1993

Preaching at church in Lima, Peru, February 1993

A few days before we left Peru, they had a big gathering for us. There was lots of food with much of it being popular local dishes. I tried a lot of different things that I probably shouldn't have. The next day my stomach was upset. I could only eat about two or three bites of food before it began to hurt and churn very badly. So I ate very little, at times only eating a few bites of bread before having to stop. When it was time to leave, we boarded a bus and traveled all night to Quito, Ecuador. I was still sick and very weak when we arrived. I couldn't eat any food that evening, and when it was time to go to the church service, I was too weak to get up. I stayed in bed while everyone else left. I slept for a while, then woke up feeling very badly, and realized I was in very poor condition. In the last couple of days, I'd had hardly any food or water. I wanted to call somebody for help, but I couldn't speak Spanish, didn't know the address of where I was, couldn't remember the name of the people we were staying with, and nobody would be home for several hours yet. I had been sick for over a week, and it felt like I was dying.

It is crazy how the mind works—sometimes really helping with logical thought process but other times totally irrational and illogical. I remember thinking how sad it was that I would die alone because I knew I would have some profound thing to say before I died, and nobody would be there to hear it. It was ridiculous the way I was thinking! Finally, I realized that I couldn't be dying with all those crazy thoughts going through my mind. I concluded that I must be better than I thought. But I did do some serious thinking and praying after all this and asking God to take care of me so I could finish up my work before heading up to Glory. By the time everyone got home, I was able to get up and eat a few bites of food. My stomach seemed to be settling.

Our next stop was in Bogota, Colombia, where I would be staying with my friend Russel Stendal for a few days. When I got there he asked me what was wrong because I didn't look so good. After explaining my stomach situation, he took me to a friend of his who had a pharmacy. After hearing the story, he gave me some pills and explained that it was probably some ameba that I picked up. The pills would take care of the ameba and restore my stomach back to normal. After a few days with them, I flew to Chicago where Betsy picked me up. Our plans were to drive back to Whitehorse. It felt so good to be back together again, but I was still having some stomach problems and back pain. When we finally arrived back in Whitehorse, I went to get my physical for the renewal of my pilot license. The doctor, who was a friend and fellow pilot, was just starting to check me over as I told him about my problem in South America. He stopped and had me lay on my back. Then he ran his finger along my lower rib on my right side. The pain was horrible. He finished the physical, then had me do some blood work, and gave me some medicine. His conclusion was right. My liver was enlarged due to infection from amebic dysentery. I learned that he had spent some years in the tropics and had seen the exact thing. After five days of intense antibiotics, I was back to normal. Thanks, Dr. Tony De la Amare!

The country of Belize was the next adventure outside of North America. It used to be called British Honduras but got its independence from Britain in 1980. Trades4Life started a trade school there near Belmopan with a goal of not just teaching trades, but faith and life skills too. Our son, Steve, along with Kent Fuller from Belmopan, were the ones starting it. I got to teach mechanics with Colin Giesbrecht the first year. We flew there for a week at a time for a total of six weeks. It was exhausting since it took almost two days to get there, our schedule was full the whole time, and was followed by a two-day return trip. We did this for six months in a row staying only a week at a time. We were interested to see if this project was really going to work or was it just a good idea but not practical.

Trades4Life 2013, Colin and I cleaning up at the end of the day

Colin and I had nine mechanic students. It was full, and at times chaotic, as we tried to teach mechanics and mentor them as they allowed us into their lives. We soon learned that these young men opened up very quickly because we were open and taught everything we could. We had torn a car engine apart and were looking at each part for wear. It was obvious that the bearings on the crankshaft had worn from not having clean oil. Contamination had worn them out fast. Everyone examined them carefully to see the work of contamination.

As we were reviewing for a test, Colin held up a worn-out bearing and asked what it was that destroyed the bearing. They knew the answer—contamination. Then he asked them what they thought would destroy their lives. After a bit they answered, "Contamination?" He followed up by asking, "What might that be?" One of the students answered, "Pornography?" We had an excellent time talking about the effects of uncleanness in our lives. One of the students pointed at me and asked, "Mr. John, do you keep yourself clean?" I had never been asked that question, and I was thankful that I could answer, "Yes." He followed up by asking, "How do you do it?" Our review for a mechanic test turned very personal as Colin and I shared with nine young men about the Grace of God working in us to be able to do what is right with a clean heart.

Me teaching an evening class at Trades4Life, February 2020

Later, I shared with them about the time I was flying from Calgary to Vancouver. It was a smaller plane so there were only two seats on each side of the aisle. I always tried to get an aisle seat and had succeeded in doing that on this flight. But the question always remains about what kind of person will be sitting by the window beside me. On this flight it looked like there were a lot of people who worked in camps, for they looked pretty rough and some were a bit tipsy. I was hoping for a nice clean person and not one that was dirty and smelly. Soon after I got seated, there was a young blond-haired girl walking to the back and looking for her assigned seat. I noticed that a lot of the rough looking guys were watching her, and I assumed they were wishing she would be sitting beside them. As she approached my seat, she looked at me and indicated that she was sitting by the window next to me. I stood in the aisle while she got into her seat.

Just as I was ready to sit back down, a guy about three rows ahead of me stood up and said, "Why is the prettiest girl on the plane sitting beside you?" I assumed that maybe he thought I was the ugliest man on the plane, but my response surprised me. Without thinking, I replied, "Because she is safe with me." That ended the questioning from him. I was impressed with how these things work out because as I started talking to the young lady, I found that she was the daughter of a pastor in Vancouver. She was returning home after spending some time making wedding plans with her fiancée. Our conversation was mostly about marriage and family. She asked some very personal questions. After the trip was over and I looked back, I was thankful and more determined than ever to keep my life clean.

Working in Belize with Trades4Life has been an exciting adventure, watching young men grow with a hunger to learn and be changed. Classes have grown, and the 2020 class was thirty-five men. We all start off the same, not knowing anyone and wondering how things will turn out in the end. While there are a few disappointments, the rewards of watching the intensity grow in these men is amazing. Included in this chapter is the speech given at graduation by Denrick Clare, one of the plumbing students. I share this with his permission. This is our work at Trades4Life from the students' perspective.

Trades for Life

God is good. I don't deserve this honor, but God is good.

Like all of us in Cabin 10, when we walked into Kindred Spirit Compound, we were all hurting. Some more than others but nevertheless we were hurting. We all made sacrifice to be here. Some greater than others, but we were all making a sacrifice nonetheless. We were in search of something better for our lives and the lives of our loved ones.

Hopefully we all found what we were looking for... progress... change in a positive direction. Personally this is what I found...

I remember being in a stalemate with myself questioning if I would be a part of Trades4Life 2020, or would I just be another thug with a dream and no means.

I had applied for the plumbing course and received no reply, so I became persistent and called but received the answer that the plumbing course is full. Oh mein, my heart sunk...there and then I decided to take the streets full force for 2020.

Strangely, as I had that thought, a text came in from Trades4Life saying I was accepted. A joy filled me up almost to tears. To me, somebody was trying to help me make a better me.

Subconsciously a voice in my mind said, "you don't belong around those people, you won't fit in, you will only be a bad influence to those youths." I was sure in my heart that I could be a better man, a tradesman even. After all, my life was being trampled down to my lowest point. I had lost a lot of friends, but I did not wish to fight back physically.

The first week, I felt like Mr. John was a mind reader. Our first life skill session was concerning change and how pain motivates change. He was hitting my emotional nail on the head. I realized then and there that this was no regular trade school.

I found myself searching my soul for answers to questions I never knew haunted my life. They were but repressed memories, and I stared into the mirror of my soul from that week and found myself with the strength to put to rest many of my shortcomings.

I had started a transformation I didn't even know was visible to others. After all it was not even visible to me. However, the first clue was when Mr. Jeremiah personally played Reckless Love for me. If you know Mr. Jeremiah, he plays his guitar and sings with his whole heart. I knew how Saul felt when David played for him...I had to run. I told him I was feeling something.

He had moved my spirit... I had to battle with my emotions that night and every day since. I felt the chains holding me fall away and I made up my mind: I don't want those chains on me anymore. Whatever or whoever was holding me had to let go. I felt free... I was at peace with myself and my environment. This does not mean that I became Jesus Christ overnight...after all, change is a timely process...There is a season for everything, and this was the highlight of my season to change.

In case we forgot the reasons we came to be a part of Trades4Life Family, weekends when we return to our homes, we are quickly reminded why we chose to make this sacrifice...because a change is needed in our lives.

Only when we are able to make a change can we then truly have appreciation for life.

This ring I wear on my finger, even though I am not a jewelry person, was given to me by my children and it has served me well as a focus point to keep my mind on the purpose of this journey.

I proudly represent the Trades4Life plumbing family. With the help of Señor Caleb, (plumbing instructor) the chemistry in Cabin 10 became a real brotherhood where we all decided... If one can, all can.

We grew in togetherness, in prosperity, in pain, in prayer and in skills as a family for six weeks. Caleb always insisted that practice makes permanent.

We practiced in theory and nobody was left behind. We practiced in our practical work, and we can all agree that something permanent has been laid in our hearts.

None of us have the same personality that we walked into Trades4Life on January 12, 2020. Especially amongst the plumbers...because...as Mr. John constantly reminds us in song...we don't have to be the same as we were yesterday.

As a class, we now have trade skills we can continue to build on. We have gained new associates who are God-fearing and business oriented. Our leadership skills have increased, and we now have a heightened drive and focus to add to our purpose in life.

A wise man once said, "The two most important days in your life are firstly, the day you were born, and second being the day you find your life's purpose."

Truthfully, I believe we have found our purpose. And if not, we will be able to walk into the future as men of skill and confidence being able to shape our own destinies pertaining to work.

We can only show our appreciation for this life changing experience. Speaking of appreciation, we would like to call on Señor Caleb to receive this small token of appreciation from the plumbing family of Cabin 10...We ask a few words from Mr. Caleb.

I end with a quote taken from John 10:17-18. "Therefore my Father loves me because I lay down my life that I may take it again. No one takes it from me, but I lay it down myself...I have power to lay it down and I have power to take it again...This command I received from my Father."

Thank you.

CHAPTER 19

Writings

"When Heroes Hurt"
Written for Victor Hesser by Grandpa John

Definition of a hero: "A man or boy admired by a great many people for his bravery"

When heroes hurt, all heaven stands.
When Stephen felt the stones from the angry men's hands,
He saw Jesus standing on God's right side.
The Glory that he saw, he could not hide.

When heroes hurt, they know they can cry.
No one understands, even though we try.
It's the pain inside that is the hardest,
These are the times that it is the darkest.

When heroes hurt, it's because the pain's been long.
"Why can't this be over and gone?"
But inside the hero there is something like gold,
Others don't understand how to get it, even though they are told.

When heroes hurt, they want to stop walking,
Get out of the race and stop all the talking.
All the words of advice, try this, and try that,
It seems like nothing more than a worn-out old hat.

When heroes hurt, the angels are sent down
To bring a life-giving gift that smooths out the frown.
The black clouds can no longer swarm,
And the sun is once again warm.

When heroes hurt, and even when they're not,
Others can see them, and their friendship is sought.
These heroes are great people, gentle and kind,
But they can't see themselves as heroes, because they
are blind.

When heroes hurt, they see themselves as lesser
Than all others; but for me, Victor Hesser
Is a great hero, and I stand in awe,
For you see, I get to be... his Grandpa.

"The Wounded Lamb" is an allegory written for 5-year-old Heidi Hesser. It is the story of her daily struggle with pain, surgeries, and problems that are impossible for a child her age to understand. It is also the story of her first understanding of Jesus' sacrifice and what He carried for us on the cross. Her very young faith—and the faith of her family—has been severely tried. She is greatly loved and cared for by her dad and mom, Steven and Jewel, brother Victor, and sisters Betsy, April, and Emme-Lee.

The Wounded Lamb"

The Shepherd was tending his flock and paying special attention to a young family of sheep. There was mom and dad and five little ones. Each one was special. Four were girl-lambs and one was a boy-lamb. This story is about the youngest one, a girl. She grew up very happy and loved to talk and sing as soon as she could make a sound. Running around and playing in the grass made her look just like all the other lambs in His flock. But the Shepherd knew something that no one else did. There were problems that no one else could see.

This lamb had been sent to the flock with a very different purpose. No one would know for a long time just what that purpose was except for the Shepherd. It would take a special family to work with the Shepherd and care for her. She would need special sisters and a brother to help as well. They didn't just make sure she had food and other care. They also spent time playing, working, talking, laughing, and praying together.

In many ways her life was just like the other lambs. She played and had friends. She also had to learn all the lessons the others learned. Sometimes it was hard to give in and just do what she was told. But she always tried.

As her problems got worse, she needed to see a doctor. Years before she was born, the Shepherd had prepared a good doctor, Dr. Green, to help her. She had to go through some very painful surgery and was wounded. Dr. Green always did his best because he, too, loved this little lamb. First they tried one thing, then another, then another, but nothing really did what Dr. Green wanted. It seemed that all she got was more wounds.

During all these times the Good Shepherd was watching and helping this young lamb so she could do what she had been sent to do. When she was put to sleep in the hospital, the Shepherd would hold her till she woke up. Oh, it was hard!

Sometimes she would cry out in bed declaring she wanted it all to stop. She just wanted go home and enjoy running in the grass again. She got so tired of the pain in the hospital: needles, tubes, medicine, wounds. There were days when she wasn't allowed to eat or even have a drink. Time went very slowly after surgery. But the day always came when she got to walk out of the hospital. She could finally join the rest of the sheep in the pasture she loved.

She had gotten to know and love many people—lots of family and many close friends. All her friends were special, but she had never gotten to know the Shepherd. He was always someone that seemed far away, so she never thought of Him much. He was just someone that others talked about sometimes.

Then one day in a song she heard about Gethsemane. The Shepherd had been there long ago. It was a very hard time in His life as He struggled to do the things His Father had sent |Him to do. She learned things about the Shepherd that she never knew. He had promised to give up **His** life so she could live. The Shepherd had let soldiers pound nails through His hands so He could hang on a cross and die. He said, "The Good Shepherd gives His life for the sheep." That is just what He did—for her. She always got sad when she would think of all the pain and wounds He had. But it helped her when she was wounded and had pain too. The Good Shepherd understood. He was always close by when she was hurting, even though she couldn't see Him.

Her family did not know how long this pain would last. But they knew that everything the Shepherd did was for a purpose, and there would be an end. Only the Shepherd knew when all this pain would end. Only He knew when all the wounds would be healed for this little lamb.

The little lamb grew and began to understand the Shepherd. Soon, she began to love Him, too. When she faced more needles and wounds in the hospital, she cried for it not to happen. She did not want to go! But she had started to understand the love of the Shepherd. He just always did what His Father wanted Him to do.

The difficulties and pain began again, but this time she chose not to run away from it. She wanted to be like the Shepherd. He had become so special to her. Her decision was made. She wanted to be just like the Shepherd, so she told him, "Whatever You ask, I'll just do it." And the Shepherd came closer and carried her because He understood.

"A Tree Finds Rest" is an allegory written for 9-year-old Victor Hesser. It is the story of his journey through multiple surgeries, much physical pain, and the trial of his faith. It is also a story of the trial of faith that his dad and mom, Steven and Jewel, and his four sisters—Betsy, April, Emme-Lee, and Heidi—have shared with him.
By Grandpa John Troyer, April 2011

A Tree Finds Rest

A great King planted a garden full of trees. Anyone could come to this garden if they wanted to see and understand the great strength and tenderness of the King's love. He gave each tree a choice. Some chose to be on their own and belong to no one but themselves. They commonly called themselves "Nick Trees" because they didn't want anyone to know they really were "Iniqui-trees." The others chose to give themselves back to the King. They didn't want to be anything but what they were created for; they only wanted to be His servants. The King called them "Son-trees."

The Nick trees were very obvious. They grew with their branches stiffly jutting out and up stiff and rigid. They were proud. They wanted others to know how strong and capable they were. On sunny days they admired each other as they stood together, straight and tall, displaying many dark shades of green. Nice words were spoken, but inwardly they all competed to be the tallest tree with the biggest branches.

Everything was different when stormy winds raged through their branches. They only thought of themselves and their own survival as the wind whipped around their trunks and through their branches. Each one stood alone with their eyes on themselves. The more they resisted the wind, the more painful it was when they were forced to bend. They hated the storms and longed again for the day they could admire their own beauty. Eventually the sun would shine, but the Nick Trees always lost some of their beauty during each storm. By the time they were old, all their beauty was gone. Only twisted trunks and shattered limbs remained. Resentment filled their hearts and sapped their strength. They had no memory of sunshine, only the storms that blew and destroyed the beauty they thought they had.

The Son-trees were quite different, so the Nicks resented them for taking up space they wanted for themselves. Son-trees always lifted their branches, wanting them to reach for the heavens, not for themselves. Their branches had the appearance of worship as they were raised gently towards the sun. At first glance, there seemed to be something wrong with most of them. Some had branches with bare spots or ends that were broken off. Every morning they all saw the beauty of the sun and looked up, thankful for its blessing that day. Every Son-tree knew he had no beauty in himself. In fact, they could only see their obvious blemishes and all the broken places that needed healing.

The same storms that blew on the Nick Trees battered the Son-trees as well. Many times they thought they wouldn't make it through the storms, because they knew how weak they were. During these times they lifted their eyes to the sun. By faith they could see it through the clouds. Because of their faith, their trunks and branches could be bent by the wind but not torn off, even though at times the pain was intense. Somehow they were getting stronger and healthier as the wind made their hearts more soft and bendable. No one could understand how this worked. It seemed to be a miraculous work of the power of the sun in their lives.

There was a time when a young tree was added to a family of Son-trees. Before he was even planted, the King knew exactly what kind of tree He wanted and where He wanted to plant it. His dad and mom knew he was to be a special tree. They often prayed that the sun would shine on him at just the right times and in the right places. They named him Vick Tree. Knowing that the storm winds would blow, they prayed that Vick would learn how to see the sun through the clouds.

The King first planted him in the Far North. He had many cousins, friends, Grandpas and Grandmas around him. Before long, his family was transplanted farther south into one of the King's gardens there. The King made sure he still had lots of family and friends. He would need them all to help him during the windstorms.

As Vick grew some of his branches had problems. At first it didn't seem like anything serious, but it was very uncomfortable for him at times. He would see different tree experts for help, and they tried many things. They pruned his branches, dug around his roots, and gave him special nourishment. Sometimes they propped up his lower branches with special stakes. Nothing helped. Vick often wondered what was wrong. Why did he have so many problems and his friends didn't? Would the complications ever end? Did anybody know what was happening? Was anyone in control? Would he ever become a strong healthy tree?

The King knew exactly what He was doing. At times He sent sunshine on Vick and his family. At other times, the strong, stormy winds blew. These were needed to strengthen his heart and to soften the hearts of his parents and grandparents. The work of the King was obvious to those who were watching. Vick tried so hard to be strong and grow. He wanted the King—and everyone else—to see that he could take his place among the rest of the trees with his strong branches.

But as time passed, it seemed that the storms grew darker and the winds more violent. During one of these times, all Vick could do was barely keep his roots in the ground. The wind blew him from side to side, twisting and shaking him in every direction. His whole family gathered around him through the storm. It looked like the storm was destroying them all! Suddenly, the King appeared beside him as the last great gust of wind nearly tore away his branches.

As the winds died down and the clouds broke open to the sunshine, Vick asked the King why He waited so long to come and stop the storm. Vick tried to explain to the King that he almost lost his branches and was close to being completely pulled out of the ground. He showed the King his broken, wind-whipped branches. He felt so sad that the King was seeing him in this condition.

The King's answer stopped all the other questions in his mind and set his heart at rest. Now he could understand as he heard the King say, "I didn't come to stop the wind, even though I knew it was breaking your branches. I stood by you in the wind, knowing that strong winds make strong hearts. I look for trees with strong hearts, not pretty branches." The King gazed deep into Vick's heart and was pleased. Vick was finally at rest, knowing that he was pleasing to the King.

CHAPTER 20

Inspirations

There have been key times in life when God would send just the right person, book, or event that would bring the perfect inspiration to motivate me to keep my relationship with Jesus fresh, alive, and real. Many times it was awkward because I often had the feeling that I didn't fit in with many Church circles or other Christian people that seemed happy and carefree about life. For a while this bothered me, but over time I found peace in being who I was made to be and in doing what I was formed to do.

The first Bible that I really paid any attention to was given to me by my Mom and Dad on August 16, 1969. This is the one I spent hours reading late at night in my cabin in the remote village of Pikangikum, Ontario. I discovered that its words washed my heart and mind. About that time, I found a poem written by Lorie Gooding. I printed it on the front page of my Bible and read it often for many years.

"Candles"
By Lorie Gooding

The world all about me in darkness I see,
And only one candle is given to me.
Each heart has a candle, if all were alight,
How their glow would combine to illumine the night.

Lord use my small candle, may this be the spark,
To set many candles aglow in the dark.
So many long candles and glowing so bright,
That I'll not be missed, when I've burned out my light.

(*The Gospel Herald*, August 22, 1961. Printed with permission.)

In the mid 1970's, I read a book by Jamie Buckingham, *Into the Glory.* This book was a big part of me getting my heart set on "serving the least" and discovering the Glory of knowing the pleasure of God in the quiet moments, alone, sensing His pleasure with me. These times never came in church meetings or crowded rooms, but always when alone with the one who saved me by His Grace and called me to follow Him. The following summary is about the book *Into the Glory* that riveted my attention and solidified my commitment to "fly into the glory."

> ...But these are the rugged people who have heard the call of Christ to come away from the glory of the crowds and comfortable living to serve naked aborigines and headhunters whose languages have never been committed to writing. Sometimes their only thanks is a brandished spear. But sometimes, far above the clouds, they

enjoy the momentary glory of looking down at the shadow their little crafts cast on the cloud-tops. Around that shadow a peculiar dispersion of the sun's rays creates a corona of light. Pilots have long called that corona "the glory" and when they finally have to descend beneath the clouds, they fly "into the glory." At the moment the plane and shadow converge at the cloud, there is a virtual explosion of light. And in a special sense for the pilots of JAARS, they do fly into the glory — the glory of serving the least of all the peoples of the earth in obedience to Jesus Christ. (Jamie Buckingham. Retrieved from https://jamiebuckinghamministries.com/into-the-glory/)

EGB flying above the clouds in southern Yukon

While I never faced a spear, I do know what it is to face violent threats and to have axes and knives thrown at me. One spring day, while walking past a log cabin, I heard someone yelling at me in anger. I looked up and watched him raise a rifle to his shoulder and begin firing. While I could hear the bullets hitting the log cabin behind me, I also heard the quiet voice of God saying, "Turn right and walk away." So I turned right and walked away while several more shots were fired.

It was never hard to understand the opposition and resistance from people who had no true knowledge of God. It was to be expected. But when the "spear" was in the hands of other Christians who opposed us when we didn't follow what they expected to be normal Christian living, it was almost harder to endure. I never could understand how, or where, so many false accusations against us came from. But through it all, I have known what it is to fly "into the glory," knowing the bright light of His Presence, as well as physically flying the airplane into that corona of light. These were wonderful times, all of them!

The book *Beyond Pentecost*, by Clayt Sonmore, came into my hands in the late 90's. I don't remember where I got it or why I started reading it, but it was another time of establishing me in the work I was to do. As I read this book, which was the third edition, I spent a lot of time on pages 183 and 184 on a writing titled "The High Calling." At the end it only says, "Author known only to God." I don't know where Clayt Sonmore found this, but I would have loved to meet and talk to this writer.

"The High Calling"

If God has called you to be truly like Jesus in all your spirit, He will draw you into a life of crucifixion and humility. He will put on you such demands of obedience that you will not be allowed to follow other Christians. In many ways, He will seem to let other good people do things which He will not let you do.

Others who seem to be very religious and useful may push themselves, pull wires, and work schemes to carry out their plans, but you cannot. If you attempt it, you will meet with such failure and rebuke from the Lord as to make you sorely penitent.

Others can brag about themselves, their work, their success, their writings, but the Holy Spirit will not allow you to do any such thing. If you begin to do so, He will lead you into some deep mortification that will make you despise yourself and all your good works.

Others will be allowed to succeed in making great sums of money, or having a legacy left to them, or in having luxuries, but God may supply you only on a day to day basis because He wants you to have something far better than gold, a helpless dependence on Him and His unseen treasury.

The Lord may let others be honored and put forward while keeping you hidden in obscurity because He wants to produce some choice, fragrant fruit for His coming glory, which can only be produced in the shade.

God may let others be great, but keep you small. He will let others do a work for Him and get the credit for it, but He will make you work and toil without knowing how much you are doing. Then, to make your work still more precious, He will let others get the credit for the work which you have done; this to teach you the message of the cross, humility and something of the value of being cloaked with His nature. The Holy

Spirit will put a strict watch on you and with a jealous love rebuke you for little words and feelings or for wasting your time, which other Christians never seem distressed over.

So make up your mind that God is an infinite Sovereign and has a right to do as He pleases with His own, and that He may not explain to you a thousand things which may puzzle your reason in His dealings with you. God will take you at your word; if you absolutely sell yourself to be His slave, He will wrap you up in a jealous love and let other people say and do many things that you cannot. Settle it forever: You are to deal directly with the Holy Spirit. He is to have the privilege of tying your tongue, or chaining your hand, or closing your eyes in ways in which others are not dealt with. However, know this great secret of the Kingdom: When you are so completely possessed with the Living God that you are, in your secret heart, pleased and delighted over this peculiar, personal, private, jealous guardianship and management of the Holy Spirit over your life, you will have found the vestibule of heaven, the high calling of God. (Printed with permission.)

After reading this over and over, I committed to this kind of relationship with God. At times failing terribly, at other times, finding extreme delight knowing the personal care of the living God of the universes. I have no regrets. Maybe this is why, still today in 2020, my greatest joy is talking about life and God with a customer in their motorhome, a close friend, or a homeless man looking for a coffee.

God also uses people. He has always had people at the right place and the right time to inspire me in the journey. About a year after we left Fort Ware, I was struggling to find where I fit and what I should be doing, because I often had a feeling that I was useless. I couldn't see that God had any purpose or work for me to do. It was a very dry, unfulfilling experience and I didn't know what to do. We had gone to a church convention in Dawson Creek, British Columbia, and a very good friend, mentor, and pastor, was there. While we were there, John Clarke, who has since gone to be with the Lord, said he would like to talk and find out how things were going for me. I will never forget his patient, listening heart as he sat and paid attention to me talk on and on about the emptiness I felt. After so many exciting years of serving the Lord at Fort Ware, now there was nothing - just emptiness. Finally, when I stopped talking, he sat up straight, looked me in the eye, and said, "It's called Potiphar's Prison; just stay there until God brings you out." That was the end of our conversation. Then he stood up and said good-bye. But a light came on inside of me even though nothing in my situation changed. He helped me see that God needed to sow some things in me before the next assignment. We moved to the Yukon about a year later and a bright, exciting time of service to the Lord began.

Sometimes the people that inspire us the most are right beside us and we don't realize the impact they are having on us. My wife, Betsy, is one of those people. Before we were married, I heard people say that once you were married for a while the "rose-colored glasses" come off and you see your partner as they really are. It was often implied that there would be disappointment when we discovered what our spouse was really like. But it has been the opposite of that in my relationship with Betsy. From the beginning, she was always more than I thought or dreamed that a wife would be. Now, after almost fifty years of marriage, she still inspires and amazes me with her life, love, and commitment. Through all our years together, she has

followed me in some pretty tough places and put up with
very difficult living conditions while raising five children.
We made our home in a total of twenty different houses.
Thankfully, there were other times when she was smart
enough, and strong enough to look at me and say, "I will not
go there," or "I will not do that." So we didn't. I am who I
am today, because of her.

Happiest together!

The following is what she wrote just before our wedding.

"One in Christ"

We are no longer two, but one.
Through the love of God it all begun.
Things don't just happen here on earth,
God has a purpose for each birth.

As small children we didn't think of Poplar Hill,
But there God led us to fulfill His will.
Working for our Master at such a place,
Helped us understand the Native's case.

We, as children of God had many things to share,
Blessings received and burdens for the work there.
It was during precious times like these,
The Spirit called us to our knees.

The power of prayer has no end,
We realized through the letters we did send,
How the Lord answered prayers each day,
Has led us together in this way.

We've experienced heartaches and sorrows,
From God's Word, comfort we would borrow.
We can say those moments were dim,
But joy and peace came only by trusting Him.

What the future holds, we don't know,
But certainly God will each day show.
There's bound to be discouragements and sadness,
But with our eyes on Christ, it can be turned to gladness.

A miracle this is to be joined together as one,
It all started when we said'
"Lord, not my will,
But Thine be done."

The above poem was written by Betsy Martin a week before
her wedding (February 20, 1971). This is what her courtship
and marriage to John Troyer meant to her.

Betsy's award-winning garden in Whitehorse

Many men have had a part of my life, but none of them stand out like the one I called "Dad." I watched and admired him while he took care of Mom during the years she had cancer; much of the time she was in bed. He would do anything that need to be done in the house, worked a full-time job to support the family, and was a dad to his children. I never heard him complain or talk about it being too hard. He gave his testimony at Fairview Church one evening, and very simply summed up some very difficult times in his life, by saying that there were times that he told God he just couldn't take it anymore. But then he would remember that "All things work together for good to those who love God," and he knew he loved God so he could trust that it would all work for good. Listening to Dad's testimony has caused me to check out my love for God more than once. God gave Dad so many blessings too. He loved and married Barbara Krabill in 1973. Together they had two children and she became our second mom. When Dad could no longer take care of himself, she gave him the same tender care that he had once given to another. Stan and Barb have inspired me and many others by the love they had for each other.

Dad and Mom at Dad's 80th birthday celebration in 2010

One of the many great blessings that I've received is getting to be "Dad" to five wonderful people: Faith, Steven, Nathan, Jewel, and Philip.

Family in 1987

Family in December 1993

Watching them grow from children to mature adults through many painful life experiences has inspired me to be faithful in everything I do, whether it relates to things eternal or the temporary things of this life. They all amaze me with their diligence and dedication as they strive for excellence in their chosen field of work. Added to all this, the eighteen grandchildren and one sweet great-granddaughter have all brought many hours of pleasure. All these have brought an added determination to remain faithful and true to the One that I met while on my knees in a church in the little town of Cairo, Nebraska.

CHAPTER **21**

Looking Ahead

There are times in life when the future looks very difficult due to the factors that are unknown. But there are also times when the future looks secure and enjoyable. Both of these conditions are based on how we see our present condition. I have heard it said, "If you want to know what your future will be, look at your past, because it will be the same unless you make some changes in your present." I have found it to be true. During the times when I was insecure and afraid, the future looked impossible and, at times, terrifying. But when I faced my insecurities and fear and found peace, it was amazing how my view of the future changed.

The main thing that brought security and hope in my life, in a wide variety of life experiences, has been my relationship with Jesus. I want this relationship to be something more than what He did for me in the past. My peace and security are because of what that relationship is today. Jesus bought me by what he did for me on His cross, so I belong to him. I am not in charge of my life, but I am responsible for it. Now as I look ahead to an unknown future I am at peace. I have learned that God has a plan for me, and even though there may be pain and difficulties here, I will make it through. The message I want to leave with you, Dannette, Katelyn, Darlene, Stanley, Betsy, Rachelle, Blake, Victor, Whitney, April, Autumn, James, Emme-Lee, Kendra, Gabe, Nicole, Heidi, Kimberly and Brielle, is this: If you want to know the most exciting, challenging, fulfilled life, put your life in God's hands and follow His plans. Your future will be guaranteed to be above and beyond anything you could dream of making for yourself. He planned the birth of each one of you and gave you a perfect gift and exciting purpose. God will take charge of your past, present and future, making you a pillar to those who look for reality.

The whole family at Fort St. John, B.C. for Christmas 2017

As you look ahead and journey into the future, your challenges and life experiences will be different than mine. Your world will not be the same as mine. None of us knows how far out our journey will go, when or how it will end, but we can know a bit about it by looking at our present. As I journey through this present life and enjoy the presence of One who is greater than me, I find satisfaction with a life full of purpose. I know that when this life is full of purpose, the life to come will also be full—total, eternal satisfaction, because the Grace given to me years ago continues its effect today and will throughout eternity. Don't hold back, live your life to the fullest in spite of adversity, and your eternity will be full of satisfaction in the presence of Jesus, the One who saved us, called us, and gave us everything we need for life.

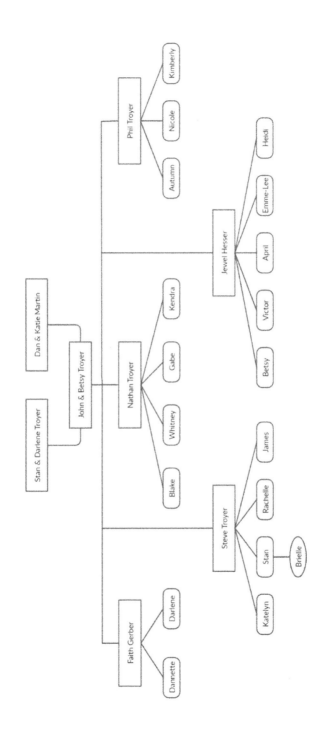

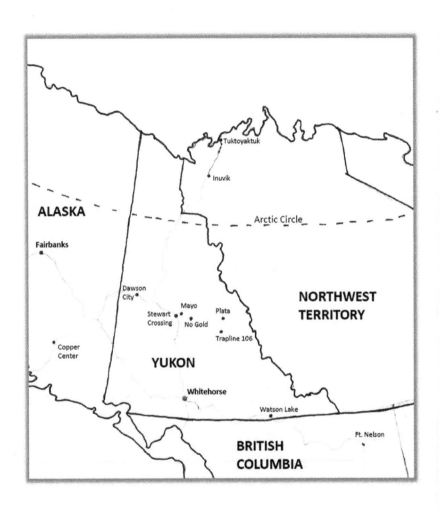